WHERE JESUS WALKED

. . . in search of Jesus Christ among the towns and villages, mountains and deserts —shrines and 'holy places' of present-day Israel.

by
David Marshall

STANBOROUGH PRESS
GRANTHAM ENGLAND

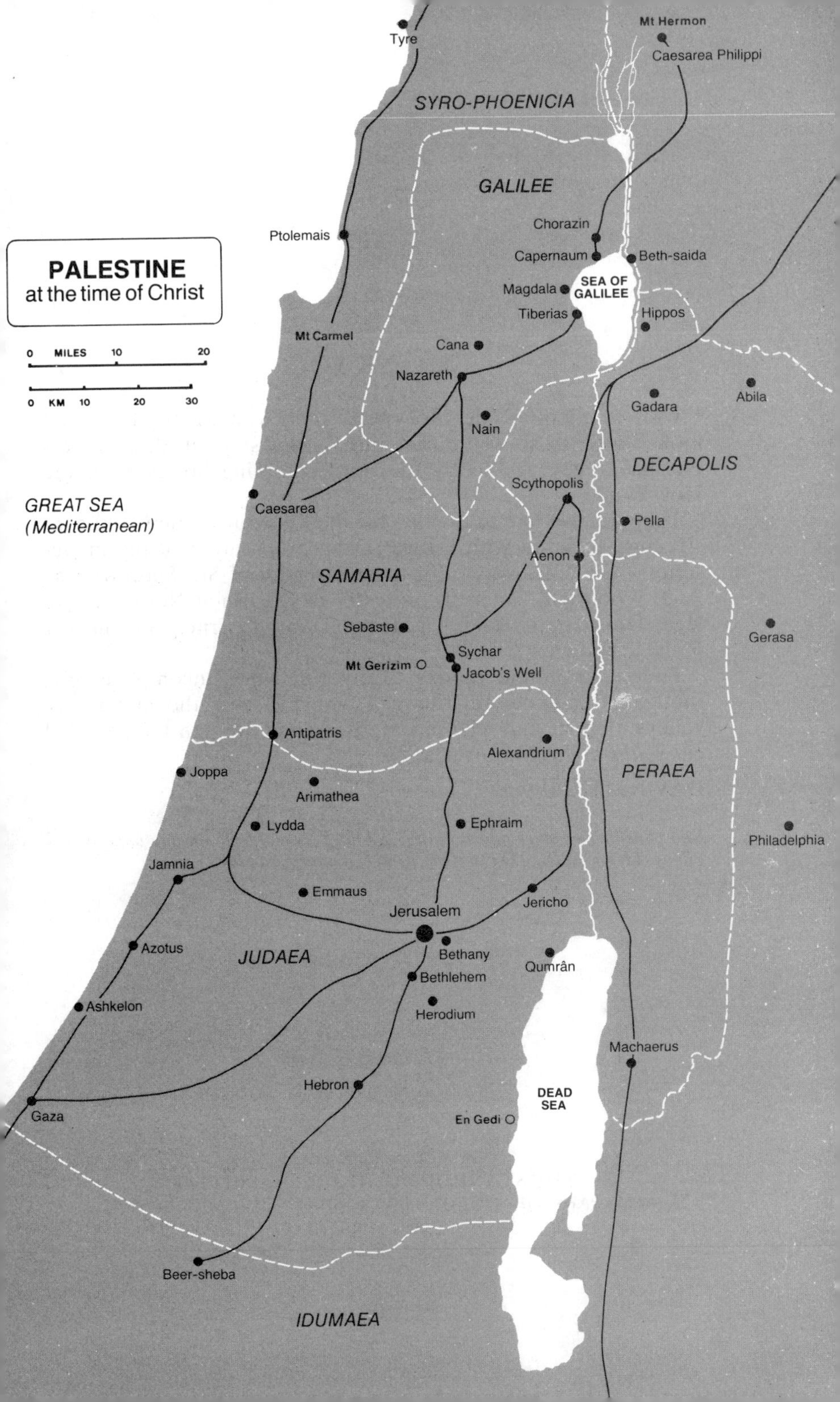
PALESTINE
at the time of Christ
0 MILES 10 20
0 KM 10 20 30
GREAT SEA
(Mediterranean)
Tyre
Mt Hermon
Caesarea Philippi
SYRO-PHOENICIA
GALILEE
Ptolemais
Chorazin
Capernaum
Beth-saida
Magdala
SEA OF GALILEE
Tiberias
Hippos
Mt Carmel
Cana
Nazareth
Gadara
Abila
Nain
DECAPOLIS
Scythopolis
Caesarea
Pella
Aenon
SAMARIA
Sebaste
Gerasa
Sychar
Mt Gerizim
Jacob's Well
Antipatris
Alexandrium
Joppa
PERAEA
Arimathea
Lydda
Ephraim
Philadelphia
Jamnia
Emmaus
Jericho
Jerusalem
Azotus
Bethany
JUDAEA
Qumrân
Bethlehem
Ashkelon
Herodium
Machaerus
Hebron
DEAD SEA
Gaza
En Gedi
Beer-sheba
IDUMAEA

THANK YOU

I wish to thank Katie McDowall and Lynn MacFarlane who looked after us so well during our various stays at St. Andrew's Hospice. They are surely the most charming hostesses in the Holy Land.

I should also like to thank – for their encouragement and constructive criticism with regard to the preparation of the manuscript – Dr. J. C. Walton of the University of St. Andrews, Dr. A. J. Woodfield, emeritus professor of English at Newbold College, Dr. Silburn Reid, Dr. Hugh Dunton, Ernest Logan and R. H. Surridge.

Finally, profound thanks to my wife who uncomplainingly, though often footsore, tramped with me over the mountains, valleys, deserts and wild places, as well as through the crowded city *souks* of this colourful land.

DAVID MARSHALL

Note: Spelling of place names varies. We have standardized on that used by Zev Vilnay, THE GUIDE TO ISRAEL, 22nd edition revised (1982).

FIRST PUBLISHED 1986

ISBN 0-904748-32-4

Printed and Published by

THE STANBOROUGH PRESS LIMITED

ALMA PARK GRANTHAM LINCOLNSHIRE ENGLAND NG31 9SL

CONTENTS

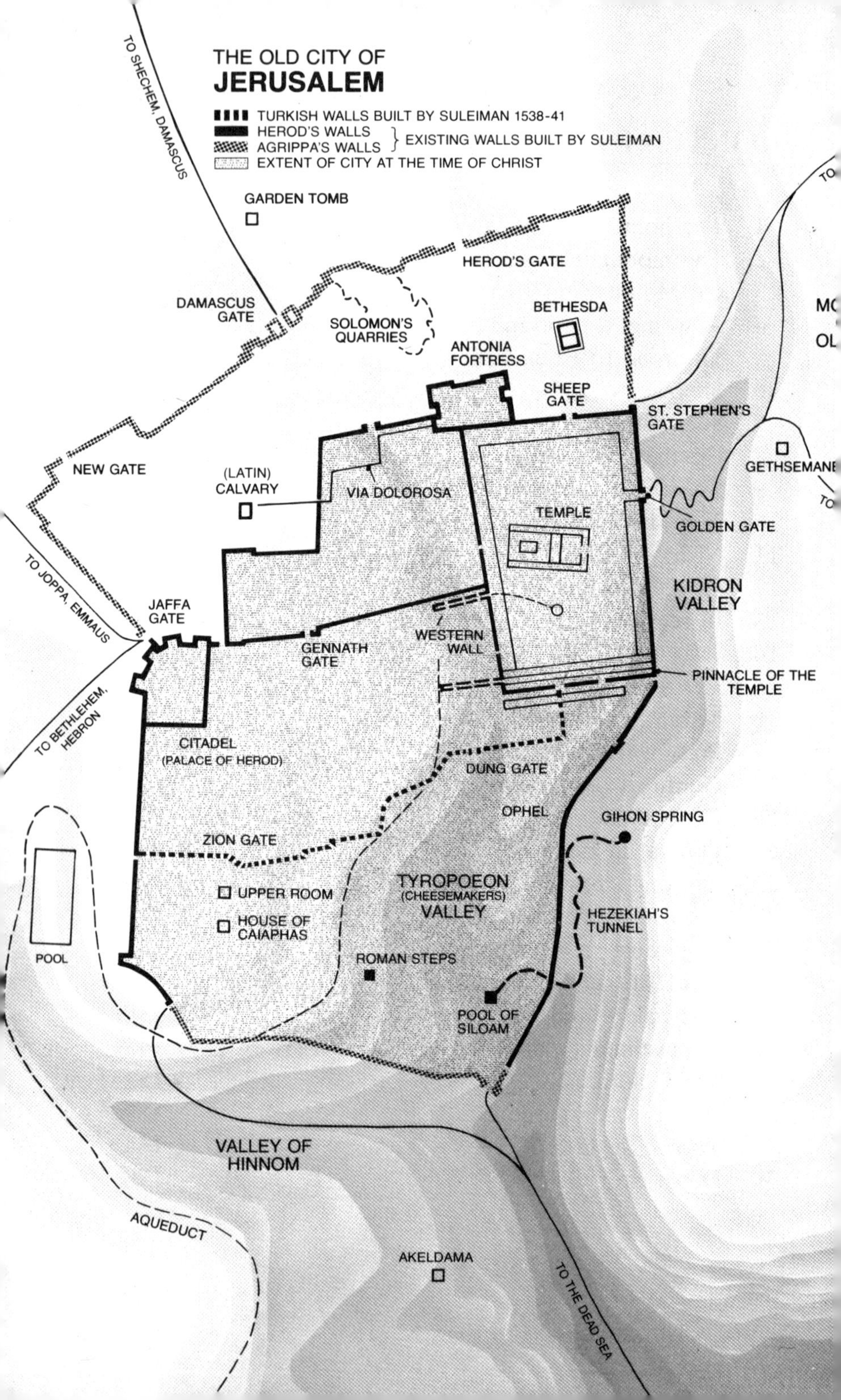
THE OLD CITY OF
JERUSALEM
TURKISH WALLS BUILT BY SULEIMAN 1538-41
HEROD'S WALLS
AGRIPPA'S WALLS
EXISTING WALLS BUILT BY SULEIMAN
EXTENT OF CITY AT THE TIME OF CHRIST
TO SHECHEM, DAMASCUS
GARDEN TOMB
HEROD'S GATE
DAMASCUS GATE
SOLOMON'S QUARRIES
BETHESDA
ANTONIA FORTRESS
SHEEP GATE
ST. STEPHEN'S GATE
GETHSEMANE
NEW GATE
(LATIN) CALVARY
VIA DOLOROSA
TEMPLE
GOLDEN GATE
KIDRON VALLEY
TO JOPPA, EMMAUS
JAFFA GATE
GENNATH GATE
WESTERN WALL
PINNACLE OF THE TEMPLE
TO BETHLEHEM, HEBRON
CITADEL
(PALACE OF HEROD)
DUNG GATE
OPHEL
GIHON SPRING
ZION GATE
UPPER ROOM
HOUSE OF CAIAPHAS
TYROPOEON
(CHEESEMAKERS)
VALLEY
HEZEKIAH'S TUNNEL
POOL
ROMAN STEPS
POOL OF SILOAM
VALLEY OF HINNOM
AQUEDUCT
AKELDAMA
TO THE DEAD SEA

WHO WAS HE?

Introduction

He lived in a country with a population of less than half a million. By any standards it was a tiny country; 150 miles from end to end, fifty miles across.

His story takes off in the most cosmopolitan province of that tiny country. Traffic from 'the four corners' passed close by the town where He was reared. Roman occupation was the great issue of the age. His home-town hills harboured freedom fighters who struck at military targets under cover of darkness. But the issue, so important to others, was of no interest to Him.

In the year of His birth there was a widespread belief common to many cultures – Roman, Greek, Persian, Hebrew – that a world Deliverer would arise. But if He was that Deliverer few saw Him as such. Not surprising. He was born in an outhouse, not a palace. Some sniggered at the circumstances of His birth. His training was of a practical nature; He received no formal education. When He left home He lived rough out of doors. He had the capacity to inspire loyalty, but knew few, if any, of the 'right people'. He shunned popularity and refused political position.

He achieved, it is true, a certain localized celebrity as a preacher-cum-healer. Short of a 'rise and rise' to fame and fortune, to the image-conscious His career was a saga of missed opportunities.

When His whispered words of wisdom began to collide with expectations He lost any mass following He might have had. Only a nucleus of His original support followed Him to His end, and one of them betrayed Him.

Early thirties, still in His prime, He was arrested. A sham trial under cover of darkness. A contrived sentence. A criminal's death.

Finis. The End.

The really remarkable thing about His story was that the end was only the beginning.

Three days following His execution a persistent rumour ran through the streets of His country's capital that He had come to life again. In circumstances in which they could very easily have been proved wrong the nucleus preached: His tomb is empty, we have seen and talked to Him, He is risen!

They had cowered in corners behind bolted doors after His execution, but they now stood fearlessly before the Supreme Court of the land, heads erect, and said: 'The Man you put to death is alive. He is God's Son. We are His witnesses.'

The nucleus became the most powerful force known to history.

Time itself is measured by this Man's life on earth. Each year is given the stamp of His authority, Anno Domini, the year of our Lord.

Napoleon, exiled on St. Helena, remarked: 'Alexander, Caesar, Charlemagne and I founded empires. But on what did the creations of our genius rest? Upon force. He alone founded His empire on love, and to this very day millions would die for Him.'

After a long, cool look at His life Phillips Brooks said: 'I am far within the mark when I say that all the armies that have ever marched and all the navies that were ever built, and that all the parliaments that ever sat and all the kings that ever reigned, put together, have not affected the life of man upon earth as did that one Solitary Life.'

From the story of His birth, life, ministry, death and resurrection, centuries of men have derived the moral, spiritual and intellectual creativity out of which has come everything great – truly great – in our art, architecture and music. The story has illuminated thousands of the greatest minds. The number of individuals who claim and have claimed that their lives have been changed, rebuilt, transformed, is utterly beyond our powers of computation.

He was either a charlatan, said C. S. Lewis, or He was exactly what He said He was. Certainly His claims do not allow us to take an in-between position. The claims He made for Himself offer us two alternative beliefs. Either He was completely mad, a megalomaniac caught in the toils of His own deceptions, or He was God come to live then die that centuries of prophecy might be fulfilled and that man might be reborn into a new spiritual dimension.

* * *

Logic dictates: *either He never was, or He still is*.

Which?

With pencil, pad, a hire car and stout footwear we set out on an adventure in the land where He had lived to find out if, after twenty centuries, we could uncover any clues. . . .

THE HOMECOMING

1

Departure from Heathrow was delayed.

The British Airways Tri-Star – chartered by the Israeli government because their national airline was on strike – was only half full.

A Pan Am jumbo jet was seen taxiing in. And soon all spare seats on our flight were taken by an influx of loud-talking, gesticulating, back-slapping American Jews.

Soon we heard the gentle thunder of the wheels on the runway and experienced the exhileration of knowing that we were airborne to an exciting destination.

We had left Heathrow at 13.55 London time. We would arrive at Ben Gurion at 19.40 Jerusalem time. The distance was 2,200 miles.

I unrolled the copy of *Time* I had brought for diversion and, with a wry smile, noticed the title page: ISRAEL A LAND IN TURMOIL.

The cacophony of voices and sounds, which always seemed to be rising to a crescendo, made concentration impossible. This was unlike any flight I had ever taken. Instead of the usual settling down in one's seat, the muffled conversations, the pretence at staring out at the cloud cover, there was more of the atmosphere of a huge old-fashioned family outing.

Groups from the front of the plane stampeded to pump the hands of beaming red-faced persons near the rear who received them like long-looked-for prodigal sons returned from a far country. Here and there groups embraced one another. Elsewhere individuals were standing up addressing animated persons six rows back or at the other side of the plane.

Increasingly I became aware of an amply proportioned elderly lady on my immediate right. She was beaming at me with tears in her eyes. Before I embarrassed myself by endeavouring to open up a conversation, an airline stewardess leant over and informed us that the lady came from Siberia, spoke only Russian and, after the ancestral exile, was on her way to the home she had never seen, Israel.

The introduction now seemingly complete the lady opened up to my wife and myself in voluble Russian. Having already heard German, Dutch and French spoken on the plane I experienced a sense of relief that, at least, no one could *expect* me to understand Russian. Of the profusion of elderly very Jewish non-English-speaking Jews who occupied the seats behind us not one spoke Russian. And, in any case, in this great mid-air family reunion, in which no one knew anyone else but all were bound by the ties of blood and a shared history, our Russian Jewess had chosen *us* as her 'long lost cousins', the only Gentiles on the flight.

Her talk was incessant and totally unintelligible. But she worked on the assumption that the more she spoke Russian the more likely we would be to understand.

What we understood of her, and she of us, of course, was not language, but understand each other we did. By the time that the cloud cover which had held over central Europe cleared and we saw Salonica and then the Island of Rhodes bathed in the late evening sunshine we might as well have been what she thought we were – long-lost cousins of the Diaspora going home to her Promised Land.

Before moon-thrown shadows on the Mediterranean and cold striking through the windows announced the onset of dark there was, it seemed to me, an unseemly rush to the front of the cabin. Then, as the Tri-Star banked, heavy, copper-coloured beams of light came in at the west-facing windows, gilding the outlines of many heads with red gold, and falling on the opposite wall of the cabin in rich, ruddy illumination.

At that point I realized that the large group of men gathered at the front were facing Jerusalem in an attitude of prayer. Like untold generations of Jews before them, including Daniel from *his* place of exile,[1] they were petitioning Yahweh in the evening. The evening, the *beginning*, not the end of the day; beginning their day with God. 'And the evening and the morning were the first . . . second . . . third . . . fourth . . . fifth . . . sixth day' until 'on the seventh day God ended his work . . . and God blessed the seventh day and sanctified it.'[2] On the seventh day too there was evening and morning, but on *that* day evening to evening – the Sabbath, ending where the first day began – the hours were sacred time.[3]

As the Tri-Star banked again, and we caught sight of the light of Yaffo (Jaffa), the rabbis' Hebrew chants took on an added poignancy. Many of these descendants of Abraham had faced Jerusalem each sundown all their lives but, until now, the holy city was a thing of imagination. Now, within a hundred miles of it, they whose ancestors had been forced out hundreds of years before, began to see the place as a dream that lived and was about to assume reality. The atmosphere was emotional. Tears were shed.

Meanwhile carnal matters occupied the minds of some. The duty-free trolley drew more attention than the rabbi.

My Russian-speaking companion came alive. To the bafflement of stewards and stewardesses, her voice querulous with excitement, she grabbed bottles of vodka, whisky and cognac. At one point I did wonder if she was of the belief that 'duty free' meant 'free'. She had, in truth, discovered *two* words of English for, when I endeavoured to negotiate on her behalf, she kissed me fervently on the forehead and said 'good man'. It then appeared that she wanted me to accept a gift of 400 Harrods' cigarettes plus bottles of vodka and whisky. How does one explain to an elderly Russian-speaker that one has no intention of expiring before one's time from lung cancer or cirrhosis of the liver? However, when she then indicated that I must pay for them myself it was easy enough to put them back with a grin. After thirty minutes of all this at least one air steward was a nervous wreck.

A few minutes later the plane was coming in to land at Lod.

Temperatures in London had been 43°F.

In the heat-felted darkness which enveloped us at the Ben Gurion Air Terminal it was 74°F.

Soon, in a sherut, we were bound up-mountain for Jerusalem.

1 Daniel 6:10, 11. **2** Genesis 1:5, 8, 13, 19, 23, 31; 2:2, 3. **3** Exodus 20:8-11.

THE MOUNTAIN CAPITAL

2

The road from Lod to Jerusalem was uphill all the way. The Arab driver of the sherut applied the accelerator as if a nuclear missile was about to fall on Tel Aviv, whose lights were receding behind us.

A dozen Europeans of assorted nationalities who had come in on different flights filled the sherut. The Yorkshire-spoken English of the lassie who occupied the back seat with us – a lone traveller, we learned, in that uncertain land – made a change from Russian. How odd to be hurtling through the darkness at Jerusalem, its very name filling our imaginations with many-splendoured wonder – and to be swapping anecdotes about a coal-begrimed town in Yorkshire.

In no time our sherut was roistering through the outskirts of west Jerusalem. After that our driver cupped his right palm over the hooter and kept it more or less constantly depressed. It soon became clear that this was standard driving practice. On the dual carriageway up to the mountain capital other traffic had not been a problem. Now it got in the way. The general idea was to drive on the right-hand side of the road. Our man, however, just made for the gaps. And we soon noticed that there were many other drivers like him.

The Continentals, garrulous for the first part of the journey, stressful as we entered the city, were decanted at a series of hotels. Our Yorkshire lass was offloaded just inside the Jaffa Gate of the Old City, as close as we could make it to Christchurch.

Traffic, we found out, could only enter the Old City by two of its gates. Even then it did not get far. The maze of narrow, terraced, arched-over alleys could, with a squeeze, accommodate a donkey, perhaps the odd mule, but they effectively choked off motor transport. We owed our access by the Jaffa Gate to Turkish deference to Kaiser Wilhelm II. When he visited Jerusalem in 1898 the Turkish authorities filled in the moat between the Jaffa Gate and the Citadel and hacked a roadway through the wall to permit the entrance of the German Imperial entourage.

Arab men stood around in the dim light inside the Gate, doubtless not quite as sinister in intent as they appeared. Large groups of luggage-laden, homeward-bound Jews settled up with a score of taxi drivers and, puffing and snorting, lumbered off down St. Mark's Street towards the Jewish Quarter. All over, family reunions seemed to be taking place. Men hugging one another, women, with joy on their faces, more restrained.

Somewhere in the Jewish Quarter was the grandest reunion of all. A family of Russian speakers was reunited with a long-lost cousin. And one Jewess of the Diaspora, whose ancestors for 2,000 years had prayed towards this city at the going down of the sun, had come home.

But *we* were hurtling down the Hebron road, across the bridge over the Valley of Hinnom and up a series of perilously steep slopes towards the Church and Hospice of St. Andrew. In a cloud of dust we shuddered to a halt at the main entrance.

The Church of Scotland are the best hosts in Israel, and dinner at St. Andrews is legendary throughout Jerusalem. We had travelled 2,200 miles to get there but, over the threshold – and we were home again. Home, *almost*. There were echoes here of an Imperial past. But, in the atmosphere, there was something of home as well as homeland, and of family as well as home.

The warden managed to be both demure and mischievous, and to combine social dexterity with genuine friendliness. Effervescent personality, calm control, mobile, expressive face, head erect, equal to any situation, Miss Katie McDowall soared instantly into my personal top ten. She set the tone. She presided, as it were, over a large family representing every conceivable Christian persuasion. The hand like a chump chop which clamped on my shoulder and spun me round for a vigorous handshake, belonged to a Zimbabwian farmer. He was in Jerusalem for a Christian parallel-festival to the Jewish Feast of Tabernacles. He believed, too, that the Last Judgement would take place in the Valley of

Jehoshephat, not half a mile from where we stood. But this in no way detracted from his sense of humour or from the *camaraderie* that pervaded the whole place, and in which he partook, handsomely.

Katie led us to our room high in the church tower. Outside the mosquito-netted windows flickered the lights of another world, fraught with secrets, with a history steeped in blood and battle, whispering of small murders in the cathedral, of prophets slain, of conquests of sultans, kings and crusaders, of a tense meeting of races, cultures and religions, of violence past and of violence yet to be – and of a Saviour slain outside the wall. St. Andrews itself was built to commemorate a battle. The capture of Jerusalem by Britain's General Allenby at Christmas 1917.

But for now all must remain mysterious and magical, and we must sleep, perchance to dream of patriarchs and kings, high priests and prophets, of apostles and the resurrected Christ whose Gospel they forsook all to preach.

* * *

The Jerusalem night air was cool. The city sits on the top of a ridge which reaches from Mount Gilboa in the north to Hebron in the south. Forty miles down-mountain *west* at Tel Aviv it would be warm, even hot. But twenty-five miles down mountain *east*, at Jericho a completely different climate zone prevailed. Jerusalem, like Rome, was built on seven hills, or 'mounts'. One such mount, the Mount of Olives, serves as a barrier to the east between the city and a vast expanse of wilderness. This lunar-like wilderness falls precipitously away towards the Dead Sea and the Jordan Valley. A downward-sloping ravine links Jerusalem with the confluence of the Jordan and the Dead Sea; the Valley of Achor, which means the Valley of Troubling.

Jerusalem is 2,500 feet *above* sea level. The Dead Sea is 1,290 feet *below* sea level. This means that in the course of twenty-five miles the land falls away nearly 4,000 feet. In Jerusalem it may be cool, even frosty at night. But in the tropical world of the Jordan Valley, only twenty-five miles away, it is hot and oppressive. The Jordan Valley represents a phenomenal crack in the earth's crust which is filled with fierce heat all the year round.

There is something arrogant and unreasonable about Jerusalem, the mountain capital, perched on ridges between the lunar-land to the east and the fertile Plain of Sharon sloping down to the west. It crouches on forty centuries of debris and dry bones. The city's base looks as if it has been shaped by the Creator with a blow torch out of hot rock. It has been said that no people would have built such a city in defiance of all the laws of prudence had they not believed themselves to be under the special care of God.

King David said, 'Jerusalem is builded as a city that is compact together.' He said, 'I was glad when they said unto me, Let us go into the house of the Lord. Our feet shall stand within thy gates, O Jerusalem.'[1] To the Hebrew 'Salem' is synonymous with the 'tabernacle' of God, 'His dwelling place in Zion'.[2] They saw the geographical location of Jerusalem as symbolic; 'They that trust in the Lord shall be as mount Zion, which cannot be removed, but abideth for ever. As the mountains are round about Jerusalem, so the Lord is round about his people from henceforth even for ever.'[3] Israel's poet king insisted, 'The Lord hath chosen Zion; he hath desired it for his habitation.'[4]

Jerusalem was home and a symbol of home. Interspersed in Prophet Hosea's denunciations of the nation's depravity was the language of a strange tenderness. 'I will give her . . . the valley of Achor for a door of hope.'[5] Even in the ravine of deepest troubling there was a door of hope. Troubling occured because of sin. That troubling would one day cause Hosea's unfaithful, runaway wife to say, 'I will go and return to my husband.'[6] And the prodigal son of any and every century and land to say, 'I will arise and go to my Father.'[7] But the troubling which *created* the door of hope was not in the heart of the runaway wife, nor in the prodigal's heart. It was in the heart of God. The 'door of hope' into the light of the Father's home and the warmth of the Father's heart – was Jesus Christ. The cross was the sinner's route from the deep ravine to Salem – peace and home.

* * *

A view of Jerusalem from Dominus Flevit a quiet chapel on the Mount of Olives. It was built to commemorate the fact that, as Jesus looked over the city in the week before His crucifixion, He foresaw its blood-soaked future – and wept.

Right: The Abbey of the Dormition on Mount Zion. Nearby are the traditional sites of King David's Tomb and the Upper Room. Below: The Hurva synagogue. The Jewish Quarter of the Old City has been largely rebuilt and includes many beautiful, modern dwellings intersected by streets and squares. By contrast the Hurva synagogue (left on the picture) has been left as a ruin. Hurva means ruin.

It was light when we awoke. Our room in the tower of St. Andrew's church overlooked Mount Zion. Beyond it were the west-facing and south-facing walls of Old Jerusalem.

Packed tight between the walls of the Old City were teeming bazaars. These overran a host of places whose names rang out from the pages of Scripture. Cranes overlooked the Jewish quarter like giraffes. Churches, synagogues, minarets and domed mosques – all mixed with the squares and oblongs of accommodation and commerce, cheek by jowl, to make up the crowded jumble of a skyline.

It was a view of which we would never tire. In the gathering vaporous dust we saw, as it were, a city gilded with the shimmer of ancient devotions. In the first of the morning it was molten gold. By night a ghostly silver.

Two thousand years BC the 'King of Salem' was also 'priest of the most high God';[8] this mountain city had long enjoyed the favour of the Almighty. On Mount Moriah, on the south-eastern side, Abraham had built an altar and 'God provided Himself a lamb'. On a nearby hill the 'Lamb of God' was 'slain a ransom for many'.[9] And *He* was of the household and lineage of David. King David had recovered the city from the Jebusites. On the hilltop of Ophel above the Gihon Spring, and just south of Mount Moriah, David had built his own city. Like Abraham, David had built his altar on Moriah, and Solomon, Nehemiah and Herod the Great their temples.

In common with thousands before us down the centuries we were pilgrims, seekers. But why, above all, had we come? For what were we seeking?

Perhaps it was for the sound of *His* footfall, the imprint of *His* presence. Among the hills and valleys, olive groves and gardens, crowded streets and holy places, where would we find Him?

1 Psalm 122:1-3. **2** Psalm 76:1, 2. **3** Psalm 125:1, 2. **4** Psalm 132:13. **5** Hosea 2:15. **6** Hosea 2:7. **7** Luke 15:18. **8** Genesis 14:18. **9** Genesis 22:2, 7-13; Matthew 20:28.

ON MOUNT ZION

3

The reality of day-time Jerusalem was more heart-expanding than the phantom palaces suggested to our imaginations by the night-time shadows and twinkling lights. Indeed it soared beyond the limits of the imagination to a further, distant realm. Small hairs bristled, the heart beat faster, nerves tingled.

Inside those ancient walls, built by Suleiman the Magnificent in the sixteenth century, among the shrines and the relics, there would be crushing disappointments. The places where we *expected* to hear the footfall of the Master, registered zero, sometimes even a negative quantity, on our 'spiritual' Richter Scale. But where we did *not* expect to find Him we almost felt Him pass.

As we walked down from St. Andrews and crossed the Valley of Hinnom we thought that we would never see anything to compare with Mount Zion and the great, fierce, proud wall that stretched to The Citadel and the Jaffa Gate. The sound to which we awoke and would awake each morning, was the toll of the bell of the Church of the Dormition. The gentle, melodious tone had sounded across from Mount Zion and echoed down the valley.

As we climbed the mount through overhanging bowers of purple bougainvillaea we looked back across the valley. We could see Montefiore's incongruous windmill, the King David Hotel, the clean dwellings of the Yemin Moshe Quarter, and even Herod's family tomb. It came as a shock to recall that this had been 'front line' territory before the Old City fell to the Israelis in 1967.

We had only just reached the top of the steep ascent when an aspirant 'guide' moved in. He was clearly an educated Jew, possibly a student. There was no point when we actually hired him. But his manner soon became instructive and we were under no illusion. A fee would be expected before we parted company.

He gave us a conducted tour of the Church of the Dormition. Information poured from him, sometimes in comical English, but he was unable to answer the only question puzzling us: why the signs of the zodiac were configured in a vast circle on the floor of a Christian church – with a symbol of the Trinity in the centre and the names of prophets and saints variously intermixed.

In the crypt we were led to a plaster effigy of the Virgin whose features were composed as if in death. There was a candle at each corner of the marble on which she lay. Only two of them were lit. Not for the last time in Jerusalem we felt that we were in the presence of a celebration of death. Above the 'death bed' was a decorated cupola ringed with paintings of famous women from the Bible.

'Catholics believe Blessed Virgin fell asleep here and went to heaven', intoned our guide. 'Protestants believe that she was buried here.'

The following day we were to visit the twelfth-century Church of the Assumption in the Kidron Valley. We descended its steps into a sepulchral chamber forested with censers, and shivered despite the warm sun outside. A Greek Orthodox priest told us that *here* the Virgin died and ascended. Another legend has it that she went with the apostle John to Asia Minor and was buried at Ephesus in the 'House of the Most Holy Virgin'. . .

Lesson One in searching for clues about Christianity's Founder: learn to recognize and chisel away the encrustation of myth and legend and look for the biblical and historical foundation beneath. It is a common fault of all but official guides that potted history, garbled Scripture and lashings of legend pour forth in one lumpy, indigestible mix.

Next our guide took us across a courtyard to the unpretentious entrance of one of the most revered holy places in the State of Israel, the tomb of King David.

The tomb was made of stone and carried silver crowns of the Torah.

The site has been revered by Jews since 1158 when it was allegedly 'discovered' during excavations preparatory to the building of a Christian church. Its credibility in the mind of the pilgrim does not improve when he is led to the floor immediately above the tomb and told that he is in the upper room of the Last Supper.

Reading the uncertainty on our faces our guide fell back on the script he reserved only for his most difficult clientele. 'Actually almost everyone believes that "the upper room" of the gospels was *somewhere* on Mount Zion or what was, in Christ's time, the Upper City. Now it is outside the city walls. Then it was inside.'

In fact the Lord and His twelve humble disciples would have felt ill at ease in this impressive columned room. It is in the age and style of the chapter house in Canterbury Cathedral.

'The Cenacle or Upper Chamber,' continued the guide, whose English improved when he seemed to be reciting, 'contains symbolism representing Pentecost as well as the Last Supper. The room is also sacred to Muslims and Jews, because it was built over the tomb of King David. It has served at different times as a Christian church, a synagogue and a mosque. There is clear evidence of this.' And so there was.

'The first headquarters of the Christian Church was in the upper room. In AD 340 a large basilica called "Hagia Zion", Mother of the Churches, was built here. In 614 the Persians destroyed this great centre of Christianity. But the "upper city" has been called Mount Zion ever since. In Old Testament times "Mount Zion" was what the Hebrews called Jerusalem itself.'

Our guide led us to the domed roof of the building and from thence up the tower of the Dormition church. Here was a perfect place for an overview of this city of modern tensions and ancient devotions. A mysterious litany of voices arose from the basilica below us. Beyond the bullet-pocked Zion Gate and into the Old City, the cloying air was alive with the sounds of many noises smashing together. TV aerials festooned the white cubes of the houses dotted around the minarets and domes.

As we looked to the Dome of the Rock and beyond to Mount Scopus and the Mount of Olives I became excited. The unfortunate guide was peppered with questions as I aimed my camera every which way and shot off a complete roll of film. As soon as he had answered one question, I had a dozen more.

In exasperation he blurted: 'I too am upcitings! When I think of these things my blood is up here!' (His hand indicated a point about six inches above his head.)

Over on Mount Scopus was the great Hebrew University, he said. Following the War of Independence in 1948 it had become a small enclave of Israeli territory surrounded by Jordan. Its liberation had come with the Six-day War.

There was the Mount of Olives, crisscrossed with paths, dotted with churches, unspoiled except for a modern hotel. Our guide was angry; the hotel had been built as a deliberate act of desecration by King Hussein during the Jordanian occupation, 1948-67.

Beyond and to the south was a great ring of lion-coloured mountains, raw, sleeping and savage. Here were the mountains and wilderness of Judea and, due south, the hills of Bethlehem. The confluence of the Kidron Valley (the Valley of the Kings) and the Valley of Hinnom (or Gehenna) was in the foreground. Each slope was dotted with shrines, rubbled buildings, excavations and tombs of unbelievable antiquity.

Fascination was everywhere. So much to be seen, explored, investigated.

We entered the city at the Zion Gate where tens of thousands had lost their lives in the recapture of the Old City. In the Jewish Quarter there was evidence of massive rebuilding. But in contrast to the frenzy of noise and activity we had looked down upon all was quiet now. The cranes and bulldozers were still and deserted. A calm had fallen on the homes of the Jews.

Our guide had already excused himself. My watch said 4.30. The streets emptied. The half-constructed buildings, wonderfully authentic, blended beautifully with their ancient surroundings – but were quite deserted, desolate.

With a little trepidation and some reverence in our tread we walked the silent streets, crossing an empty square to pass the Hurva synagogue. In sharp contrast to the frenzy of the day the peace of our surroundings entered our own souls.

In some homes the women were completing the final preparations for the evening meal and for the Sabbath. Business or study or grafting to feed the family, all of it was over for twenty-four hours.

The next twenty-four-hour period, sunset to sunset, was sacred time. Time sacred to the things of the spirit, sacred to the worship of God, sacred to the family.

We saw the families gathered around the table for the evening meal and for evening prayers.

As 5pm approached we climbed the city wall. A large red drop of sun lingered over the western skyline, and then dripped over and was gone, and the sky was brilliant over the spot where it had gone, and a torn cloud, like a bloody rag, hung over the spot of its going. And dusk crept over the sky from the eastern horizon, then darkness.

Each window showed a light – and a family gathered in prayer.

As we hurriedly made our way back to St. Andrew's a bearded latecomer made for an open door. Before he entered, he turned and said: 'Shabat Shalom!'

'Shabat Shalom', I replied.

And my mind jumped to the apocalyptic passage in the prophecy of Isaiah. At a time beyond time and in an earth unearthly, cleansed of the curse, 'It shall come to pass, that from . . . one Sabbath to another, shall all flesh come to worship before me, saith the Lord.'[1] All this in another Jerusalem, another Zion.

1 Isaiah 66:2, 23.

A SPRING, A POOL AND A TUNNEL

4

The day had worked itself up into a real boiler. Heat was shimmering from the tarmac. But we were resolved to go out in search of the Gihon Spring.

It was a pleasure to escape from west Jerusalem. A squealing, honking tornado swept around its streets for all the day and much of the night.

But the Siloam Road was the domain of the donkey. The occasional camel sped proudly, silently, purposefully by. Much less frequently taxis careered through, boiling clouds of dust behind them, sending people and poultry scurrying for cover. But the donkeys munched on, unmoved.

We picked our way through the dappled light and shade of the narrow lanes of Silwan. We were in the Kidron Valley now. The great south-facing wall of the old city and the silvered dome of the El Aksa high above us appeared arrogant and overbearing. Silwan's seedy streets were silent. We missed the steady obligato of hammers and the brow-crimping rumble of the pneumatic drill, more or less continuous in Jewish areas.

But if the Jews were building for a great tomorrow, the Arabs of Silwan were determined to make the most of opportunities today afforded. And out of the silent hovels emerged a horde of Arab males of all ages who saw in us a limitless source of income.

'Ride my camel. Eighty shekelim . . .'

'No. He make camel run. Make you pay two hundred shekelim to make it stop. Buy my pictures.'

'Ride my donkey. Jesus ride donkey, *you* ride donkey.'

'You no ride my camel, so have picture taken with you on camel. Cheap.'

An intelligent lad with an armful of what looked like wooden penny-whistles hoved up. 'You buy my flute . . .'

'OK. No get on camel. *I* get on camel. I Ali Baba! You see me on TV. Yes? Films? Many times. You stand here. My son use your camera, take picture.'

This seemed a good compromise. But the outlay for the services of his camel, himself and his son – thrashed out in earnest barter – still lightened our pockets by quite a bit.

'Hey! Hello! Hello! You buy my flutes! You no play? I give you lessons!'

'Bah! Eengleesh! Feesh an' cheeps!'

Disheartened, the adults tailed off to lay siege to a cash-laden Texan setting up a tripod topped by a Hasselblad near an unattended donkey.

The children stayed with us.

'OK, Eengleesh, where you wanna go? I take you – anywhere! . . . Gihon Spring? Not here. You mean Spring of Blessed Virgin. Blessed Virgin come for water.'

But even thus renamed, the spring proved elusive for him. He left with his (modest) tip without having located it for us.

By now we had seen signs to the Pool of Siloam and resolved to follow them.

But the images of Silwan remained. Not the extrovert hucksters. The images in the shadows. Old men with the hollow eyes of hermits. Old women with creased, dried-walnut faces. Faces shrivelled by years of attrition and by the staleness of poverty.

At the Pool there was one souvenir shop. We entered it. Colleagues who had visited Israel three months earlier had made friends with the family who were its proprietors. They had taken photographs of them. We had the developed photographs with us. The delight of this Muslim family was unbounded, and humbling. Soon they were refreshing us with cool drinks; and one son was detailed to conduct us to the Gihon Spring – and lead us through Hezekiah's Tunnel.

It was not difficult to see why we had missed the spring. Of enormous historical importance, it has no memorial marking the spot. There was just the spring itself – fenced inside a school playground with a perilously-built, two-storeyed building almost over it.

Inside the walled city, Jerusalem seemed to worship every

relic of her antiquity. Out here, beyond Suleiman's walls, antiquity was worn with disconcerting carelessness. But, before Suleiman, before the Wailing Wall, before Pontius Pilate, before the various temples, before Roman, Median, Persian and Babylonian conquerors – was the Gihon Spring.

The name means 'gushing'. That's how King David found it in 1048 BC. That's how it is today. The warrior king came upon its welcome refreshing after a forced march from Hebron. At that time the spring and Jerusalem were in the hands of the Jebusites. The spring was their greatest asset. To tap it they had sunk a shaft from inside their fortified city to the water source outside.

That fact gave David his strategy of attack.

'And David said on that day, "Whoever would smite the Jebusites, let him get up the water shaft." '[1] Joab took up the challenge and the city fell. All eleven acres of it. It became David's capital. The ark of the Lord was brought there and, at the Gihon Spring, David's successor, Solomon, was anointed by Nathan the prophet and Zadok the priest.[2]

* * *

As we followed our Arab guide down the dank stairway to the iron grill, beyond which was the tunnel, the glories of former days were not apparent. We rolled our trousers up and lit our candles, then ventured into the 1,750-foot tunnel hacked and chiselled by men out of solid rock during the reign of Hezekiah, 728-699 BC.

After Solomon's death had come the division of the kingdom – Judah and Benjamin around Jerusalem in the south; the ten tribes of Israel around Samaria (Sebaste) in the north.

At the time of Hezekiah's accession in the South, the Assyrians were in the process of dismantling the Northern Kingdom. Soon the chill, menacing shadow of Sennacherib fell over Jerusalem. ' "This is what Sennacherib king of Assyria says," taunted Ninevah's envoys. "On what are you basing your confidence, that you remain in Jerusalem under siege? When Hezekiah says, 'The Lord our God will save us from the hand of the king of Assyria', he is misleading you, to let you die of hunger and thirst." '[3]

Hezekiah's answer to this menace was both spiritual and practical. He destroyed idolatrous worship and, clothed in sackcloth, spread Sennacherib's demands before God in the temple, praying for deliverance.[4] Then, recognizing the importance of a water source to the city under a prolonged siege, he covered the Gihon Spring and, in one of the great works of engineering in ancient times, had his army of pick-wielding men hack their way from the Gihon (*outside* the walls) and from Siloam (then *inside* the walls) – and meet in the centre. They succeeded. The Assyrians were defeated.[5]

* * *

Trudging through the water, ankle-deep, knee-deep and, at one point, close on waist-deep, in this 2,700-year-old tunnel, it was a comfort to hear voices both ahead and behind. This was especially true when, thanks to one of the air ducts thoughtfully provided by Hezekiah's engineers, our candles began to blow out. The black water seemed menacing and when the tunnel, at first a comfortable six feet high, was so low as to cause us to bend almost double, claustrophobia seemed to be setting in.

To reach the Siloam end and have the bright sunlight replace the blank sightlessness of that seemingly endless tunnel, was an experience almost comparable to that of the man Jesus sent to wash in the Pool. In answer to the legalists seeking to trump up a charge against Jesus arising out of the miracle, the testimony of the now sighted man was: 'One thing I know, that, whereas I was blind, now I see.'[6]

1 2 Samuel 5:8, RSV. **2** 1 Kings 1:43-45. **3** 2 Chronicles 32:10, 11, NIV. **4** 2 Kings 19:14, 16. **5** 2 Chronicles 32:4, 30; 2 Kings 19:35, 36. **6** John 9:25.

THE ROAD TO BETHLEHEM

5

It snowed at Christmas the first year we were in Bethlehem.

On 25 December, as the Latin patriarch and his procession were welcomed by the Mayor of Bethlehem, and the carolling of the choirs of many nations rang out from scores of churches, the snow was descending, silently, stealthily.

When the pilgrims had emerged from their midnight Christmas Eve service they had seen the first of the snowfall. When they awoke in the morning it had possessed the landscape, softening the skyline of flat-roofed houses and geometric shapes of domes, minarets, towers, crosses and mosques which make up the intense jumble of the town. Had the shepherds come with haste to see the thing which had come to pass *that* night of Christmas, as they did on the first Christmas, their footfalls would have been traceable in the snow – from Shepherds' Fields to the manger bed.

But snow is unusual at Bethlehem, an event that occurs once or twice a century. Though in the weeks before Christmas the little town often cowers beneath skies filled with cannoning thunder.

As our hire car rounded the bend and began its downhill judder, however, Bethlehem was as usual: in blistering heat that had all but scorched every vestige of colour out of the surrounding hills.

Christmas was still nine weeks away and the season that saw the special birth at the crossroads of time is more likely to have found Bethlehem thus. Shimmering days and cool nights on bleached terrain. Not the lush of spring nor the sharp of winter.

Dodging stray rocks and the more cavernous pot-holes we hurtled downward on the town between shaggy, dirty sheep grazing among the nettles on either side of the road.

The car came to a halt, after a close shave with a camel, outside the first souvenir shop in Manger Square, a courtyard away from the Church of the Nativity. The Arab proprietor, whose acquaintance we had already made in Jerusalem, took a swift step back and looked distinctly unimpressed with our driving. After a quick recovery he beckoned us into an impossibly narrow parking space between two crumbling high walls, but off the road.

Leaving a son who wanted to study computers in charge of the shop, he took us over to what he announced was the oldest Christian church in the world.

Remove the bell tower and it would look more like a fortress.

When Christianity had emerged from the catacombs following the Edict of Milan in AD 312 this was one of the first sights identified as holy. Justin Martyr, born in Nablus in AD 100, knew of a grotto in Bethlehem where Jesus had been born. The Emperor Hadrian knew of it too, for, to repress Christianity AD 132-135, he dedicated a grove to Adonis over the Grotto of the Nativity. This desecration enabled Christians to home in on the spot. Evidence dating from AD 220 indicates that, Grove notwithstanding, Christians visited the grotto in the belief that Christ had been born there.[1] It was Constantine's mother, Helena, who, on a pilgrimage to Palestine in AD 326, gave instructions that a church should be built.

Our Arab guide told us that, of the three entrances, two had been bricked up in the Middle Ages, and the third and highest portal lowered so that all must stoop to enter. The inscription read: 'Lower yourself, you proud one, if you want to approach God, who for your sake came to us as a child.'

Inside there was a central nave, two lines of monolithic columns, and beyond them two aisles. To the left and right of the altar and beyond the columns two stairways led down to a labyrinth of caves beneath the church. The first cave we entered contained a fourteen-pointed silver star set in cracked marble. Around it were the words: 'Hic de Virgine Maria Jesus Christus natus est', 'Here Jesus Christ was born of the Virgin Mary'.

Nearby, hewn out of the living rock and now faced in marble, was the manger.

Our guide urged us on. Business was spoiling. But a large

group of white-robed Nigerian nuns bent low in devotion. An American matron, mummified in heavy make-up, shrieked: 'Hey, they're prayin'! Get a shot of them, George, while they're prayin'!' We passed into the Cave of the Innocent Children, in memory of Bethlehem's children who fell victim to Herod's paranoia.[2] Then on into Jerome's cave.

The Dalmatian priest Jerome arrived in Bethlehem from Rome in AD 386. In a cave adjoining the Cave of the Nativity he translated much of the Holy Scripture from the original Hebrew and Greek into Latin. The Latin Vulgate was the only Bible available in Christendom for a thousand years. A statue outside the neighbouring Church of St. Catherine, built by Austrian Emperor Franz Josef in the last century, commemorates his achievement.

We re-emerged by way of the Church of St. Catherine into the twentieth century. Our guide returned to his shop promising to take us out to Shepherds' Fields later in the day. We had time to absorb and analyse what we had seen and learned.

The bull-dozers of our imagination were shoving and tearing with all their force to shift the debris of twenty centuries from this hallowed spot. And the shutters were down to close off the sights and sounds of the moment. We were reaching back to a time when, on the tick of prophecy, a thin cry pierced the blue cold of midnight in Royal David's overcrowded city. A child born amid the deep and dreamless sleep of this tiny town wherein the hopes and fears of all the years were met . . .

. . . Joseph and heavily-pregnant Mary had travelled sixty miles from Nazareth so that, in the fullness of God's time, the Son of the Highest could be born here, in Bethlehem. If not in the very spot marked by tradition, then within a stone's throw in any direction.

* * *

The hour was late of their arrival. Nevertheless long lost (and almost forgotten) friends and relatives were greeting each other. Now when was the last time . . . ? The Passover or the Feast of Tabernacles? It was one or the other! But all were heedless of the pregnant woman on the tired donkey.

They were at the inn. All was activity, inside and out. Bundles were being carried in. Beasts led to shelter. The two late-comers were ignored.

Now where could that innkeeper be? Mary, still seated on the donkey, felt uncomfortable. She knew it wouldn't be long. Wished they'd hurry!

And hurry they did – about their own affairs. The innkeeper's honeyed deference was reserved for the VIPs. But who was that bearded man with the rustic Galilean accent? His wife outside, waiting to be delivered, did he say?

The innkeeper was finally induced to leave his honoured guests for a moment.

'Sorry, full up!' he said.

'But my wife . . .'

He simply shrugged: 'Sorry, no room. In a hurry. No time to spare. All rooms taken. There's only the stable!'

Hence the birth in a manger, with the beasts of the field. In no great pomp and circumstance of an earthly prince; Messiah's first bed, on straws as sharp to His tenderness as the thorns to come after.

In the stable was darkness, and darker animal shadows; animal warmth and cow-breath. There was urgency and tension. Scurrying movements. Pain in cramping knots. Then the thin cry; and Mary calling weakly to Joseph on the hardened stable yard outside, 'Come, Joseph. Come and see Him!'

* * *

We had passed out of the courtyard of the Church of the Nativity. Across Manger Square, past the incongruous modernistic fountain. Car horns were blaring. Donkeys were braying. The Arab proprietors of the little bazaars in this all Arab town were insistent. Police whistles blew.

. . . If an everlasting light indeed shone in these dark streets, it went unnoticed. If the noise of angels indeed sounded above the thin cry of the Man-child, it went unheard. For the whole earth, like this tiny town, was swallowed up in the deep and dreamless sleep of ages, and eternity was lost to the world of time and politics and barter and brass tacks.

Nothing has changed.

1 Origen, Contra Celsum I, 51. 2 Matthew 2:16.

SHEPHERDS' FIELDS

6

We had left Manger Square behind and were wandering aimlessly, if a little nervously, in Bethlehem's back streets.

In these tiny, twisting alley-ways there was a wierd admixture of the ancient and the crassly modern; interlinking houses made from wattle and daub – topped by TV aerials.

The air was alive with many noises. Incessant horn-honking from the traffic-choked streets nearby. The noise of camels, hollow, guttural, as if from the depths. Herds of tourists, wearing ridiculous green, yellow or pink identifying hats, with impatient couriers, pushing, shoving and managing to be generally *gauche* in just about every western language. Arab boys with hand-carts heaped high with fresh bread trying to make their way down the terraced alleys and shouting 'Hello! Hello!' when they really meant 'Make way!' The amplified calls of the muezzin, wailing out from loudspeakers high up on the minarets; now turned up to full blast in keeping with the resurgence of Islam.

There was the unmatchable arrogance of the Israeli soldiers, with machine-gun slung over one arm and a girl tucked under the other. And there were the dark, lowering stares of hate and contempt from many of the Arabs. Here, as everywhere in Israel, there was an edge in the atmosphere; a small but definite whisper of trouble.

A police raid on an out-of-town, well-tucked-away refugee camp yielded the cameras, lenses, films and sundry other valuables stolen from our photographer's car as he had looked out over the Dead Sea three months earlier. We made arrangements for their shipment back to Britain.

We returned to the souvenir shop next to the Church of the Nativity, 'King David's Store'. Our Arab guide was ready to take us to Shepherds' Fields. He asked if we would mind if he drove. A German professor came with us, occupying the spare seat in the car.

Used to the narrow, pot-holed, winding roads and steep,

unexpected inclines, our guide drove confidently. We arrived at Shepherds' Fields in a cloud of dust.

The entire area appeared to be littered with monastic ruins. Some of them dated from as early as the fourth century. But under the Church of the Angels was a vast shelf of rock and, beneath that, opening onto the hillside, a cavern, clearly a one-time night holding area for sheep. From the cavern's mouth, where shepherds would have built fires on cold nights, was a wonderful view of a fertile valley, with Bethlehem atop the far slope and Jerusalem high on a distant mountain.

The fertile valley sloping up to Bethlehem earned the town its name, the House of Bread. Contrasted with the barren Judean mountains to the east, and on the horizon the mountains of Moab, purple in the rays of the setting sun, the valley and plain of Bethlehem would have seemed rich indeed. A veritable bread basket in a barren land.

The famine in the days of Elimelech and Naomi must have been exceedingly severe to have made Moab appear in any way desirable. It requires no stretch of the imagination at all to envision Ruth gleaning at the time of the barley harvest on Bethlehem's plain. The plain, still called 'Fields of Ruth and Boaz', is unchanged since these ancestors of Jesus, thirty long-lived generations back into the Old Testament, enacted their love story. Perhaps this story was in the minds of Mary and Joseph as, a few hours BC, they descended the heights of Mar Elias towards Bethlehem. Bethlehem, the House of Bread, about to bear the Bread of Life which a man may eat and never die.

There would be paining on their downward journey as they passed the tomb of Rachael; Rachael who wailed in Ramah for the children of her children's children who would perish by the swords of Herod's soldiers.

But on the night of the birth it was all bright stars and angelsong.

The many-splendoured birth went by unmarked by men of substance. Only shepherds who camped between the limestone peaks keeping watch over their flocks by night, heard the angels sing. Only wise men from Persian lands afar starled, turned their faces into the suffocating, penetrating,

D. LAWSON

Bethlehem from the roof of the Church of the Nativity. The oldest church in Christendom, this fortress-like structure was built over a warren of caves. One of them is the traditional site of the birth of Jesus. Modern Bethlehem is a noisy town thronged with tourists and populated by Palestinians, some Christian, some Muslim.

D. LAWSON

From the Mount of Olives a view of the walled city. Masonry dating from the vast platform constructed by Herod the Great on which to build his sumptuous temple forms the lower part of the facing wall.

throat-drying simoom wind of the desert – and headed for Bethlehem's stable.

And whether they knew it or not both kings and shepherds saw in that stable a wonder to outshine the vaunted seven wonders of their world. The Living God had enshrined His glory in a tiny cubicle of human flesh – suffused with blood, structured by bones, intertwined with veins, threaded with nerves – and He was laid in a manger.

In that birth in an outhouse of an overcrowded city Eternity stepped into Time, visible and invisible combined, spirit and flesh converged, God and man were brought together. On the tick of prophecy and in the destined place and context of events, need, personnel and circumstances, the Son came to earth to declare the Father. And came as a tiny, supine baby. Born as we are born.

In that vulnerable form was housed the fullness of the Godhead bodily. Holy God was wholly flesh; and wrapped in swaddling clothes. Eyes accustomed to observe the earth from end to end could not focus on the faces of the visiting shepherds. Hands that fashioned the earth and stars could hardly grasp His mother's finger. The 'voice that spake and it was done' alternately cried and gurgled.

For 'the Word was made flesh and dwelt among us' that we might behold His glory. 'Not in flaming sun nor flashing jewel does He shine in human hearts.' God does not reveal Himself in the thunder of the earthquake or in the mushroom cloud; but in the simple features of a human countenance He shines, and through a still small voice He speaks, so that 'our gaze is all transfixed – and faith is leaping out to grasp Him'.[1]

1 G. T. Bull, *God Holds the Key*, page 27.

SUCH A NIGHT

7

Night-time in Jerusalem is not like night-time elsewhere. There is never a time between dusk and dawn when one could stop, listen and pronounce, 'The world is asleep.' Jerusalem is a city that never sleeps.

The streets are seemingly never totally empty of traffic. Music from the open-air theatre not far from the old railway station remains on the air, a symbol of the city's determination not to close down. At times the night traffic seems to roar. On one memorable night it seemed that the entire Israeli army, complete with tanks and heavy artillery, was rumbling by, and that the eerie, space-age police sirens could be heard from all quarters of the city. On the following morning we discovered that the large Sabbath-worshipping Baptist church had been burned down. By young Jewish extremists, it was said.

At 5am when it seems that this city might be about to sink into slumberland, delightful church bells ring out from Mount Zion, and the sound of the muezzin blares from the old city, calling the faithful to prayer.

Galilean nights have their own atmosphere. When the human night-life of Tiberias begins to subside, there are always the sounds of the army of scrawny cats, the constant rhythm of the crickets and the weird sound of the night birds high in the trees. The first cockerel crows at 3am as if impatient for the dawn.

Walk down to the shore of Galilee in the moonshine, the wind soft, shy as a girl, there will be heard the wash of the fishing boats on the lake and the occasional shout from the darkness from men who pursue the trade of Peter, James and John. Every movement on the water is matched by the indolent chasing of wavelets round the rocks of basalt.

On one never-to-be-forgotten night in Jerusalem we lay abed to the sounds of Leonard Bernstein conducting Tchaikovsky from the Sultan's Pool beyond the Hinnom Bridge.

We came to full consciousness with a start as the 1812 Overture crescendoed and, in place of cannon-fire, the Jerusalem sky was filled with a brilliant kaleidoscope of fireworks.

That was in early May; part of the anniversary celebrations for the State of Israel. When the nights are turning towards Christmas, fresh, with glittering, pendulous stars, there is the sharp of frost in the mountain capital. And, over the hills of Bethlehem, chilling winds, occasionally the shunt of thunder and rolling cataracts of rain. Shepherds and sheep are down from the exposed slopes, in the warm of shelter.

Thus it was in a more temperate season, perhaps in the mellower air of an October midnight, that the Son of God made His appearance at the hinge of the eras. We walked Bethlehem's hills in that season and wondered. We thought of the angels who sang here and the star that shone here. The desert journey from Persian lands afar, of wise men. . . .

'Now when Jesus was born in Bethlehem of Judea in the days of Herod the king, behold, there came wise men from the east to Jerusalem, saying, Where is he that is born King of the Jews? For we have seen his star in the east, and are come to worship him.'[1]

The night sky fascinated the ancients as it fascinates us. Bright comets, with tails half across the heavens have been painted over cribs by a legion of artists. And, true enough, the belief was current at the time of Christ that such night sky phenomena accompanied the great events on earth. A brilliant comet appeared after the assassination of Julius Caesar in 44 BC. Another bright comet appeared seventeen years before the turn of the eras. The next dazzling comet came in AD 66 at the time of Nero's suicide.[2] But there was *no* comet in the year to which, thanks to Luke's historical data,[3] we can pinpoint the Bethlehem birth. Because of the miscalculations of a monk, Dionysius Exiguus, commissioned to draw the BC/AD line working backwards from 533, the birth of Christ was Before Christ! Four years BC, almost certainly in the last year of the reign of Herod the Great.

No comets then; so from whence came the star?

Johannes Kepler calculated that in 7 BC a 'new star' occurred when Saturn and Jupiter had a rendezvous in space, a 'nova' outshining other stars. But Luke's identification of the Roman Caesar at the time of Christ's birth, of the governor of Syria who completed the census and the details of Herod the Great's part in the story, as well as his historical accuracy elsewhere,[4] tend scholars to the 4 BC date.

So if 'the star of Bethlehem' was not a comet or a nova, then what?

Men like to cram the infinite inside the parameters of finite calculation, scale God down to their own size. The God who created the planets of a universe so vast that our own solar system must be considered a tiny corner of it, also created the laws of boundless mathematical complexity which govern their unerring course. Given this state of affairs, our attempts to give God 'credibility' by placing the star that led the wise men in line with our fragment of information about the universe are at best lovably eccentric.

Perhaps the clues are in the story; 'a multitude of the heavenly host'.[5] Offloading from our minds the images drawn from attempts to represent this phenomenon on canvas, and dwelling on the fact of God, we might well draw the same conclusion as a nineteenth-century writer that the 'star' was, in fact, 'a distant company of shining angels'.[6] And, dwelling on the fact of a God who, for love of sin-riddled man, became a Man to effect man's salvation, we need not be embarrassed at having reached such a conclusion. It ties in with the facts.

In 'the East', perhaps Persia or Parthia as it was then called, the wise men had been studying Hebrew prophecies about the coming One. The Magi were members of a wealthy and ancient order of high-born intellectuals. The origins of their order were in ancient Babylon where the Israelites had, for a part of their history, been held as a conquered people. Old Testament Balaam, though once a prophet of God, was counted among the precursors of the Magi.[7] Significant this; for Balaam's prophecy of Messiah had taken the form of these words, 'There shall come a Star out of Jacob, and a Sceptre shall arise out of Israel.'[8] Hence it was natural that, having made their calculations from the prophecies of Daniel that the time was right, they should have looked for a star.

But the strange thing is that the dither of expectation

caught by the Magi was felt throughout the ancient world at the turn of the eras. The Jews, said Josephus Flavius, had the belief that 'about that time one from their country would become governor of the habitable earth'.[9] That was to be expected, but the reverberations that were felt in Rome come more as a surprise. Tacitus says, 'There was a firm persuasion . . . that at this very time the East was to grow powerful, and rulers coming from Judea were to acquire universal empire.'[10] Suetonius wrote, 'There had spread all over the Orient an old and established belief, that it was fated at that time for men coming from Judea to rule the world.'[11] In the very year that Christ was born, Caesar Augustus, who had already made himself a god, declared himself to be 'Saviour of the World' and Virgil, the Roman poet, was writing his Fourth Eclogue, The Messianic Eclogue, about the golden age just dawned.

But only 'wise men from the east', star-led, angel-driven, and camel-borne, offered oblation in Bethlehem's stable. Strange, when Augustus was 'god' and 'Saviour of the World', beyond dispute *ruler* of the world; why not worship *him*, rather than the latest and lowliest of his subjects, born just in time to be among the millions numbered in his census? Had they seen, these 'wise men', what the Jews had failed to see? Seen, as the Romans could not see, that the 'golden age' would be ushered in by this the latest, lowliest of Caesar's subjects? The golden age of God's grace, salvation through God's Son, born now of a virgin? Seen the great reversal of roles that would come? Jesus, through centuries unborn reigning over men's hearts and minds – when Augustus's kingdom existed only in history books and rubbled ruins?

1 Matthew 2:1, 2. **2** Werner Keller, *The Bible as History*, page 329. **3** Luke 2:1-3. **4** Luke 3:1, 2; John Drane, *Jesus and the Four Gospels*, pages 26, 27. **5** Luke 2:13. **6** E. G. White, *The Desire of Ages*, page 60. **7** ibid., page 59. **8** Numbers 24:17. **9** Josephus Flavius, *Wars of the Jews*, vol. 6, pages 4, 5. **10** Tacitus, *Histories*, vol. 5, page 13. **11** Suetonius, *Life of Vespasian*, vol. 4, page 5.

DEATH AT THE JORDAN

8

The Allenby Bridge, barely fifty feet wide, spans the Jordan near the traditional site of the baptism of Jesus. Here the stream coils its last miles towards the Dead Sea, thickened with mud.

On one side of the bridge is the kingdom of Jordan. On the other side is West Bank Territory, still in dispute between Jordan and Israel.

A few miles away is Jericho, the oldest city in the world, built in the lowest spot on earth. To the east are Jordan and the mountains of Moab. To the south, the Dead Sea. To the north are the Jordan Valley and Galilee. To the west is the Wilderness of Judea, a weird and wild expanse of barren, moon-like mountains and valleys.

In this wilderness John the Baptist preached the coming of Messiah. Men and women came out from Jerusalem, Jericho, and even south from the populous settlements around Galilee to listen. He called them to repent and then baptized them in the Jordan.

First came *confession*. The 'OK-on-the-outside' man confessed that under the religious whitewash was a mass of filth. The unbeliever confessed that he had refused the gift of faith because he was scared of God's high standards. The masses confessed selfishness and sensuality. The soldier, the fact that his profession had served as a cover for terrorizing the poor. They confessed to God, and to one another. On Jordan's banks words of apology and forgiveness were exchanged. Peace was born in minds previously bruised and bleeding from civil war. Durable peace.

Second came *change*. Years later Peter would speak of *repentance* as a gift.[1] Paul would assure those who read his letters that *faith* was a gift.[2] James, like John the Baptist, would insist that, after these gifts had been received there had to be change. Lives had to be seen to have taken new aim.[3]

John did not believe that there was anything holy about the

muddy waters of the Jordan. Baptism was a symbol. It meant death and burial as far as the past was concerned; and resurrection to a new and better future.

But John repeatedly gazed over the heads of the crowds, knowing that one day Someone would emerge by comparison with whom he was unworthy, a forerunner.

'Then Jesus came from Galilee to the Jordan to be baptized by John. But John tried to deter him, saying, "I need to be baptized by you, and do you come to me?" Jesus replied, "Let it be so now; it is proper for us to do this to fulfil all righteousness." Then John consented.'[4]

* * *

Jesus had torn Himself away from the carpenters' shop in Nazareth. He made for the place where John baptized near Jericho. John's far-away gaze fixed on Him, and the man who did not quake before monarchs shrank from Jesus. These publicans and sinners, these soldiers and common people – had every need to repent, confess, and be forgiven. But there was surely no such need for Him, 'holy, harmless, undefiled'.

'Jesus replied, "Let it be so now; it is proper for us to do this to fulfil all righteousness." '[4]

The Jordan itself was a symbol. It originated in the vast acreages of pure, undented snow on the summits of Mount Hermon. The beauty of its earlier course to, through and beyond Galilee was symbolic of man as the Creator had made him, in His own image. But *these* troubled waters, hurrying on to the Sea of Death, represented sin-cancered man, terminally sick. With death-deserving, sinful man, Jesus now formally identified Himself. 'God made him who had no sin to be sin for us, so that in him we might become the righteousness of God.'[5]

To follow the footsteps of Jesus is to follow those footsteps into baptismal waters. In this rite His death, burial and resurrection are symbolized. By being baptized *He* identified with our sins. By being baptized *we* identify with His righteousness.

* * *

There is a universal striving for inward peace and inward

cleansing. So why do so many fail to follow the footsteps of Jesus into baptism? Do they confuse baptism with what has come to be known as 'christening'? Have they so far lost sight of what is symbolized by baptism that they are confused over the mechanics?

Those who understand Greek have no problem with the mechanics. The Greek word behind the word baptize is *baptizo*, literally 'to immerse under water, to immerse completely'.

John baptized '*in* the River Jordan',[6] '. . . because there was much water.'[7] After His baptism Jesus came 'up *out* of the water'.[8]

'Have you forgotten that all of us who were baptized into Jesus Christ were, by that very action, sharing in his death?' asks Paul the apostle. 'We were dead and buried with him in baptism, so that just as he was raised from the dead by that splendid revelation of the Father's power so we too might rise to life on a new plain altogether.'[9]

Only baptism by immersion could symbolize death, burial and resurrection.

Jesus told His disciples to go and teach and baptize all nations.[10] And the record shows that they did.[11]

Church historians agree that for centuries after Christ, immersion was the ordinary method of baptism. In many parts of Christendom it continued to be so until the fourteenth century. Elsewhere it died out in the eleventh or twelfth centuries. When it died it was replaced with the sprinkling of infants and the symbolism was lost. An infant could not repent, die to an old life and be resurrected to a new.

Baptisteries can be found in the pre-fourteenth century churches and excavations in France, Italy, North Africa – even Palestine. Under the Church of St. Joseph in Nazareth the modern visitor is shown around the ruins of a Byzantine church where he will see a full-sized baptistery.

* * *

It is difficult to approach the traditional site of the baptism of Jesus today. It is the meeting place of two seemingly irreconcilable enemies. Forces representing long centuries of hatred stand face to face.

But in the beautiful country, where the Jordan flows south from the Sea of Galilee, the tensions seem far away. After the hard drive north along the sub-tropical Jordan Valley – past ghost towns, scenes of desolation and small communities where eyes flash anger – the pilgrims' baptismal site near the kibbutz of Kinneret exudes peace and tranquility. Here, secluded among the trees, Christians from many countries come to be immersed, as Jesus was immersed, in the waters of the Jordan. We have watched many such baptisms there. As the sun drops behind the mountains west of Galilee and the brief dusk begins, still they come – as once they came to be baptized of John. And they rise from the waters, faces – African, Asian, Spaniard, Italian, staid English – radiant with the 'newness of life' which Christ offers all who enter His kingdom of grace.

* * *

The most urgent problem each one of us will ever have to face is the one in our mirror. The fundamental problems we face are sin, sorrow, guilt, judgement and death. And basic to all is the sin problem. Sin is a reality that breaks hearts, blights homes, robs heaven. Sin is a madness in the brain, a poison in the heart. It promises nectar; it gives gall. It promises silk; it gives sackcloth. There is no empire without it, no country without it, no street without it, no heart without it. It is a cancer eating away at our minds. Major surgery is called for. Solve the sin problem and you have solved the rest: sorrow, guilt. . . .

Tackling the sin problem requires more than a change of environment; more than education, psychology or political utopianism can offer. The sinner needs more than the outward trappings of religion. He needs cleansing, and through cleansing – death to an old life and resurrection to a new.

Jesus said: 'Except a man be born of water and of the Spirit, he cannot enter into the kingdom of God.'[12] Then He personalized it: '*Ye* must be born again.'[13]

Man needs power from without to cleanse him.

Man needs power from without to give him life.

He is dependent upon Another, even One who slept the sleep of death – and, awoken from it, destroyed the power of death.

New life is found through the three central acts of Christianity, the death, burial and resurrection of Jesus Christ – symbolized by baptism.

1 Acts 5:31. **2** Ephesians 2:8. **3** James 2:14-18; Matthew 3:8. **4** Matthew 3:13-15, NIV. **5** 2 Corinthians 5:21, NIV. **6** Mark 1:4, 5. **7** John 3:23. **8** Mark 1:8-11. **9** Romans 6:3, 4, Phillips. **10** Matthew 28:19, 20. **11** Acts 8:26-39; 16:30-34; 8:12. **12** John 3:5. **13** John 3:7 (italics ours).

THE WILDEST SPOT ON EARTH

9

To be lost in the wilderness of Judea is a fearful experience.

We had left Bethlehem behind and its intense jumble of yellowing dwellings, domes, minarets and towers was lost to view. Beyond Shepherds' Fields we were in 'bandit country'. We were looking for Herodion, Herod's mountain-top fortress where his body was buried in a golden bier. But we were near the refugee camps where men lurk who rob strangers in the cause of nationhood.

The signs were down.

One wrong turning.

Our tiny car was hurtling along a road built on a knife-edge ridge through an endless, terrifying, leonine landscape. The caverns were vast, their depths so far below as almost to be lost to view. The hills were capacious, some made of endless miles of smooth, barren rock. Others violent, jagged.

Sudden full turns of the wheel this way and that, sharp applications of the brakes kept us skittering on the road, just.

This was the most forbidding place on earth; as bald as a blister. But bedouins lived in goats' hair tents on the inhospitable slopes. On donkeys they led sheep along fearsome defiles. Where was their water, their food?

Eventually all around, as far as the eye could see, there was a savage moonscape of gaping wadi and harsh ridges.

I jumped on brake and clutch. Billowing dust the car came to a stop at the edge of a precipice.

We had driven miles with no signs of life, apart from distant bedouins. Suddenly the car was surrounded by a clamour of grasping, grabbing, jostling Arab children. By the time the road had cleared enough to enable me to turn the car, every loose article in the vehicle – pens, paper, souvenirs, canned drinks, packed food, *anything* not inextricably attached to us or the car – had exited through the open windows.

Two or three hours later, dehydrated and gasping, we shuddered to a halt at the first roadside cafe in Hebron.

* * *

God took forty years to train Moses on the back of this wilderness. Here the Baptist preached. To the moon-mountain wilderness, not of this world, Jesus withdrew following His baptism to be tempted of the devil forty days and forty nights.

* * *

From no point does the wilderness look less hospitable than from Jericho. Jericho, rooted in a barren desert, is a fantastic eruption of fertility fed by the fresh water of a spring.

Our first visit to Jericho was at a time of political tension. At an army checkpoint a bicycle-riding Arab youth spat at us as Jewish soldiers searched the car. It was unsafe to tarry.

Our second visit followed a state visit by Her Majesty the Queen to the Hashemite Kingdom of Jordan. The Arabs of Jericho could not have been more hospitable. We felt we had the freedom of the city as we walked the palm-lined streets. Everywhere we were greeted with 'God save the Queen!' Never had watermelon and pitta bread tasted sweeter than at the Palestinian restaurant where we stopped to snack. And, a little down the road, we became firm friends with an Arab family who ran a fruit shop and insisted on sharing their meal of white (goats' milk) cheese and falofel.

Then they pointed us in the direction of the Monastery of the Temptation. And we were back in the wilderness.

They called the monastery Quarantal, from *quarante*, forty, commemorating the forty days Jesus fasted in the wilderness. Catching sight of it from a dusty promontory just west of Jericho the monastery appeared to be a part of the perpendicular rock face that plunged 1,200 feet from the heights of the wilderness to the Jordan Valley. Even on closer inspection the thin ribbon of buildings seemed to cling most precariously to the wall of the canyon.

Associated from the fourth century with the Temptation monks had, at first, cowered in caves here. We do not know who built the first structure in this most unlikely of sites – perhaps it was the Crusading Knights Templar. The present structure was built between 1875 and 1905 by the Russian Orthodox Church.

Why early Christians chose this site as the place of the temptation is not, at first, clear. The wilderness of Judea is the backbone of southern Palestine; thirty-five by fifteen miles of blistered, peeling limestone glowing with heat like a furnace. Only up there, on the ledge, overlooking the 'fertile plain', the oasis of Jericho, the rugged mountains of Jordan and the Dead Sea to the south, we were reminded of the temptation in which Satan took Jesus to a high place and, having invited Him to survey 'the kingdoms of the world', offered them to Him in exchange for worship.

Then as we explored the caves which honeycombed the limestone Jebel Quarantal, and examined the peculiar loaf-like rocks littering the edges, we remembered that other temptation – cruel in the extreme to try on a Man empty and faint with fasting – 'Command that these stones be made bread.'

But the final temptation was elsewhere. 'He brought him to Jerusalem, and set him on a pinnacle of the temple, and said unto him, If thou be the Son of God, cast thyself down from hence: for it is written, He shall give his angels charge over thee.'[1]

Some Christians believe that this 'pinnacle of the temple' was the south-east corner of the wall of Jerusalem where Herodian masonry still rises many feet above ground. This belief originated in the days when Jerusalem was in ruins and this corner of the walls stood out like a pinnacle.

* * *

Jesus had heard God's words of approval following His baptism. In the wilderness He had withdrawn to plan His campaign, to choose His methods. By rejecting the temptations He rejected the way of selfishness, sensationalism, power and glory, and accepted the way of the cross. Jesus had deliberately retired to this desolate place for forty days to wrestle with the problem of how He could win the souls of men. It was just the *beginning* of a long battle. It was at its fiercest in Gethsemane. It found its culmination in the cross. The story of the temptation ends by saying that the devil left Jesus – *for a season*.

The forty days began with the baptism, a symbol of the new birth.

The 'arising from the water' of baptism by immersion is symbolic of rising to new life through the power of the Spirit. But the new birth, conversion, is no guarantee of freedom from temptation.

When the devil tempted Jesus in the wilderness there was nothing within Jesus that was evil to which he could appeal. Not so with the born-again Christian. At conversion the Christian is headed in a new direction, but he may still fall a hundred times a day. 'The old nature' is not taken away at conversion; it is imprisoned as the Christian looks to Christ, and for as long as he looks to Him. When the Christian ceases to look to Jesus the old nature takes over and temptation scores victories.

To the born-again Christian the New Testament offers a dangerous pilgrimage. The devil is terrified, on the run; but he still arranges rock-falls, unexpected precipices – and lots of interesting reasons to back up or divert. 'I know that nothing good lives in me . . .', said Paul the apostle. 'For I have the desire to do what is good, but I cannot carry it out. For what I do is not the good I want to do; no, the evil I do not want to do – this I keep on doing.' Paul reached desperation point with this constant struggle with sin. He cried out, 'What a wretched man I am! Who will rescue me from this body of death?' Then he answered his own question: 'Thanks be to God – through Jesus Christ our Lord!'[2]

The triumph of Jesus over temptation was total, and was sealed on Calvary. On Calvary our sin was nailed to His cross. He carried our failures on His shoulders, that we may wear the white robe of His righteousness on ours.

In the way that leads to the City of God there are no difficulties that cannot be overcome through trusting in Him. There are no dangers which we may not escape. There is not a sorrow, not a grievance, not a human weakness for which

Jesus has not provided a remedy. The trouble will never be greater than is for our benefit. The temptation will never be so overwhelming that we cannot have victory. We have a mighty Helper. But if at any stage we look at ourselves we wonder how we could ever be saved. If at any stage we look at Him we wonder how we could ever be lost.[3]

* * *

As we drove towards the sunset up the steep Jericho to Jerusalem road, the wildness of the evil-favoured hills and wadis surrounded us. But the sunset never disappeared from view, though the road beneath us was at times rough and uncertain. We thought of Psalm 63, according to the King James Bible, 'A Psalm of King David, when he was in the wilderness of Judea'.

'O God, thou art my God; early will I seek thee: my soul thirsteth for thee, my flesh longeth for thee in a dry and thirsty land . . . . My soul followeth hard after thee: thy right hand upholdeth me. But those that seek my soul, to destroy it, shall go into the lower parts of the earth. . . . But the king shall rejoice in God.'[4]

1 For the story of the Temptations read Luke 4:1-13. **2** Romans 7:14-25, NIV. **3** See E. G. White, *The Ministry of Healing*, page 249. **4** Psalm 63:1, 8, 9, 11.

TREASURES IN DEAD SEA CAVES

10

From Jerusalem 'the mountain capital' to Jericho 'the lowest city on earth' the road falls away precipitously. Over twenty-five miles we lost 4,000 feet following the route of the 'certain man' who 'went down from Jerusalem to Jericho, and fell among thieves'.[1]

The shade of the Inn of the Good Samaritan was welcome. Our faces were glowing. Sweat was running in rivulets, flooding the eyes, drenching shirts, gathering in the small of the back. Sandalled feet were bloodied, the sharp desert sand caking everything, acting like grit to raw flesh.

As we pressed on we imagined, without difficulty, that behind every boulder were murderous bands of brigands. We looked forward to rounding that bend in the mountain track beyond which would appear, far below in the Jordan Valley, the oasis of Jericho. It seemed long in coming. Every few yards we needed a swig from our water bottles.

Once in Jericho we were rested and refreshed by our Palestinian friends. Then we set off, this time by car, over the flat, battle-scarred terrain south of the ancient city. Past an army check-point – machine-gun-toting soldiers poking around the car – then east towards the Allenby Bridge, before reaching it a swift right – and we were skirting the shores of the Dead Sea, wide, blue, beautiful and restful.

A further right turn brought us to Qumran. A wall of mountain, like a massive cliff, fronted the Dead Sea. Between the 'cliff' and the sea were the ruins of the Essene Monastery. Nearby, part of the sheer 'cliff', were the caves where the Dead Sea scrolls were discovered.

From where we stood the caves appeared like holes in a rock face, totally inaccessible. Overzealous pilgrims had lost their lives trying to reach these caves, and now they were out of bounds. For centuries they had given no hint of their

A. R. RODD

The Church of the Beatitudes built on the slopes of the Mount of the Beatitudes which overlooks the beautiful, north-western shore of the Sea of Galilee. It is likely that Jesus preached the Sermon on the Mount from these slopes.

The Church of the Annunciation, a modern basilica built high above the bazaars and crowded streets of Nazareth.

treasure. Until an eventful day in 1947. A bedouin shepherd boy, in search of his goats, idly tossed a pebble into one of the caves. He heard the sound of crashing pottery. His discovery began a most exciting archaeological drama. He had stumbled on the first of the Dead Sea scrolls.

In the months that followed bedouins fairly swarmed over the area, supervised or unsupervised by archaeologists, combing every nook and cranny, every crevice, for more precious manuscripts. They were not disappointed. Soon the Dead Sea scrolls numbered hundreds.

The scrolls were the work of the ascetic Essene community, part of a Jewish *dévot* sect contemporary with Christ.

Following the discovery of the scrolls the Essene monastry was excavated. A Jewish archaeologist permanently based at the site gave us a conducted tour of it.

The monastry had been a self-sufficient community. There were workshops, a vast kitchen, a water supply system, a library, places of study – and a chapel. Adjacent to the chapel was a baptistery. We were shown a copper urn dicovered at the site containing 500 coins that helped to date the settlement to the time of Christ.

Central to the excavation was the Scriptorium. Here the Essenes had spent their lives transcribing the holy Scriptures, the main purpose for their seclusion. Desks had been found, and inkwells – with dried ink still in them! The ink in the inkwells had been analysed and compared with that used on the scrolls and had been found to be identical.

Our guide told us the story of the Essenes as it had unfolded through the years of digging and discovery.

Following the fall of Jerusalem in AD 70 they had fled to the table-mountain stronghold of the Zealots at Masada. Prior to their departure they had carefully prepared their scrolls, inserting them in distinctive urns, each with an equally distinctive 'cap'. The urns had been placed in dozens of the caves that honeycomb the mountain face.

Having thanked our learned guide we moved on along the Dead Sea road from Qumran to Ein Gedi, an oasis in the wilderness with palms and olive trees. Temperatures here were higher than we had ever experienced. There were hundreds of cars. Scores of brown-to-black bodies floated on the salt sea.

From Ein Gedi we followed the escape route of the Essenes to Masada. Warned of the intense heat at the top of the table mountain we were careful to cover our heads and to provide ourselves with plenty of liquid refreshment. We took one of the lifts to the top of the mountain.

The views of the Dead Sea and the salt flats to its southern side were unbelievable. Masada, as the carefully preserved ruins clearly indicated, had been a complete, walled city on a mountain top, almost the size of old Jerusalem.

Looking down we saw in outline the camp of Roman General Silva. We also saw Silva's ramp, built by Jewish slaves from Ein Gedi, and used to capture tableland city. After a harrowing siege the Romans had entered – only to find evidence of a mass suicide. Such was the end of both the Zealots and the Essenes of Qumran. Only a handful of women and children who had escaped the carnage were left to tell the tale to history.

The Essenes could have had little in common with the Zealots. The latter were political fanatics who would rather die than be captured by the Romans. The Essenes were studious ascetics. What both groups had in common was an absolute dedication to the ideal of Judaism. The Essenes died in the comforting knowledge that their precious Scriptures were hidden where the Romans would never find them. In the providence of God they had been hidden so well that their discovery did not come until a time when, as never before, the accuracy of the Scriptures was being questioned. The manuscripts had been hidden in the certain knowledge that God, in the fullness of His time, would lead the right persons to them. The effect upon the world of their discovery in 1947 could hardly have been more dramatic.

We returned to St. Andrew's in Jerusalem. On the following day we gave the car a rest. On foot we trekked across the modern city. Our route took us up Ben Yehuda, a wide, impressive precinct lined with Jewish eating houses and shops. Around the outdoor tables the quaintly and inappropriately attired Ashkenazi Jews, of European descent, mixed with the Sephardim, Jews of Oriential origin.

There were men who could have walked straight out of a nineteenth-century ghetto, and young ladies who would have been perfectly at home in the most fashionable boutique in West London. Everywhere there were clusters of off-duty soldiers, all uniformed, all armed.

Our walk eventually took us past the Monastery of the Cross, then on to the Knesset, the parliament building.

By now we were making sense of snatches of conversation we had caught on Ben Yehuda. There had been talk of the 'hamseen' wind. As we stood by the Minora temperatures dropped dramatically, clouds came in from the west, the wind freshened and there was a scatter of rain.

Under darkened skies we walked down the hill to the object of our expedition: the Shrine of the Book. We asked for an explanation of its curious shape and were told that it was fashioned after the tops of the vessels in which the Dead Sea Scrolls had been found.

In the dimmish light of the multi-levelled, circular shrine we examined the scrolls. We spent precious moments poring over the most priceless find of all: the Isaiah scroll. The experts in ancient Semitic script, after careful examination, reached the conclusion that this, along with the other copies, was made before or at the time of Christ.

This conclusion was of vast importance.

The manuscript is in all essentials the same as the book of Isaiah in any Bible today. Inescapable evidence, this, that the Bible has not been altered in its journey down the centuries. One authority summarized the importance of the Dead Sea scrolls thus: 'The Christian can take the whole Bible in his hand and say without fear or hesitation, that he holds in it the true Word of God, handed down without essential loss from generation to generation through the centuries.'[2]

The Dead Sea scrolls; just another fascinating chapter in the history of this fascinating Book. People have been pilloried for reading it. Men have been burned for translating it. Others have been jailed for expounding it. It has been banned and burned in countries scared of its influence. A secret network exists to smuggle it under the Iron Curtain.

The man who first began to translate it into English – John Wyclif – was hounded by the government most of his life. After his death his body was exhumed and burned. The next man to attempt an English translation – William Tyndale – was forced to flee the country. In Germany, as he proceeded with his task, he was shadowed by agents working for three different governments. With the project near to completion, the authorities moved in, broke up the type and came within a hair's breadth of capturing him. He escaped in a boat along the Rhine under cover of darkness. A few years later he was arrested in the Netherlands, strangled and burned.

The Bible has been lampooned, ridiculed, denounced, vilified as no other book has. The critics have attacked its factual accuracy; the characters and nations whose activities it records have been laughed off as 'mythical'. But under the fierce glare of scientific enquiry and archaeological research its assertions have been authenticated as facts. Time and time again its critics have withdrawn blushing. The Book was right. The critics were wrong.

A few yards below the subsoil, the Middle East is apparently replete with layer upon layer of artifacts waiting to provide mute, though eloquent, testimony to its detailed accuracy. Those artifacts, the dry stone walls, the archways still magnificent though ravaged by the aeons, those tablets and parchments – in conference and through the tools of modern science and the analysis of sharp minds, have verified the Book in such a way that faith senses that behind it stands the presence of the Great Dispenser of the Years.

Portions of the Bible have been translated into more than 1,300 languages. Since 1800 it is estimated that 2.5 billion copies have been printed and circulated. In a single year fifty million Bibles were produced in the United States alone. Each year approximately £4.1 million are spent on Bibles *in Britain*. £6.3 million pounds' worth of Bibles are exported from Britain each year.

But statistics are misleading; and never more so than in this instance. If the Bible is a best-seller, it is the world's *least read* best-seller.

And why?

Are we content with it as a talisman or a good luck charm?

Does the stress and grist of modern living and the canned fantasy dispensed by the TV companies crowd it out?

Or are we afraid that, between its covers, lies a wisdom that discerns the end from the beginning, and lends meaning to the journey from cradle to grave; a window on origin and destiny, time and eternity?

Are we afraid that the One who inspired the minds and the experience of the forty men who wrote it might have something to say to us?

The Bible is a 'God-breathed' book. It is more than an accurate history, an enthralling story, a sublime philosophy; it is a living, throbbing power able to change men, spiritually, physically and mentally, making them new men in Christ.

The inspiration of the Bible is self-evidencing. Anyone who studies the Old or New Testament with a desire to know God will soon be convinced of its inspiration. One such person, after making this discovery for herself wrote: ' "I needed help, and I found it in Jesus. Every want was supplied, the hunger of my soul was satisfied; and now the Bible is to me the revelation of Jesus Christ. Do you ask why I believe in Jesus? Because He is to me a divine Saviour. Why do I believe the Bible? Because I have found it to be the voice of God to my soul." '[3]

Through the Book and the Man in the Book we, in the circling eddy of life, can know a firm anchorage. Our horizons can be expanded. Our lives can be changed. And this is why men have been prepared to be pilloried for reading it, burned for translating it and jailed for expounding it. It is the Bread upon which Life depends.

And in 1947, under attack from all sides, vital authentication came to light in Dead Sea caves of its changeless accuracy.

1 Luke 10:30-37. See John Wilkinson, *Jerusalem as Jesus Knew It: Archaeology as Evidence*, pages 32-43. **2** Sir Frederick Kenyon, *The Bible and Archaeology*, page 81. **3** E. G. White, *Steps to Christ*, page 112.

NIGHT ON OLIVET

11

We were on the Mount of Olives and night was falling.

Twelve hours earlier we had been standing on the same spot, the sun ascending behind us. We had watched the early-morning mist rise from the floor of the Valley of the Kidron forested with small olive trees, seen the shadows flee away from its tomb-clad, west-facing slopes, watched the sun burst against the great wall of the old city, dazzling the eye as it struck the gold Dome of the Rock. We had seen the blocked-up Golden Gate. Donkey traffic had begun to enter St. Stephen's Gate. And the city, cased in by those ancient walls, had come to life.

Now we were watching the same scene against the golden march of sunset in the western sky. Black shadowing obscured the life of the squares and bazaars and courtyards of the old city. We watched car lights on the road to the south of the city walls, traffic moving with all the headlong impetuosity of frozen lard flowing uphill. The sky's dark shipping pressed closer and closer, as if all the clouds had come to harbour. And the last vestige of day melted out of the sky, leaving the permanent structure of night.

The paths that criss-crossed the Mount of Olives became mysterious. But we could pick out the churches, floodlit among the thick growth of trees. The Basilica of the Agony, by Gethsemane, on the Jericho road. The exotic onion-domed Church of Mary Magdalene. The Tower of the Ascension atop the mount. The Church of the Pater Noster below it. Strangely apart, the Chapel of Dominus Flevit where the Lord wept.

As we walked slowly over olive-clad inclines we watched the moon wading deliciously through shallows of white cloud. The olive trees and the earth around us were moon-dry. The shadows were black without shading, and the open places white without colour. The night air was cool and sweet. We drank it thirstily and recalled a conversation with a Dominican monk held earlier in the day at Gethsemane. 'Jesus never slept in the city', he had told us. 'In the winter, if not in Galilee where it stays warm, the Master would have stayed in Bethany. But for most of the year He and the disciples would sleep out on these very slopes, sometimes with a camp fire for company. When night fell there would be a place of privacy to which He would repair to eat, sleep – and introduce His disciples to the great mysteries of the Kingdom of God.'

It was on a night like this that a dignified figure left the Temple precincts by the Golden Gate, descended the valley, crossed the Brook Kidron and purposefully made his way to the night-time retreat of Jesus.

Nicodemus was a prominent Pharisee in the Sadducee-dominated Sanhedrin. The Pharisees had been outraged by the caustic words of John the Baptist, uttered in full hearing of the people. But, as a reformer among the Pharisees, Nicodemus may have seen in Jesus a potential ally against the Sadducees, worldly, corrupt, materialistic, collaborators with the occupying power. Under cover of darkness, away from prying eyes, he was out on a mission to find common ground with the new Rabbi in a theoretical discussion.

Moving silently between the trees on the terraced, lower slopes of the Mount of Olives, Nicodemus would have been totally unaware that he was about to learn, from the lips of Jesus, and be the first to learn, the very essence of the message He was on earth to preach.

Like every Pharisee, Nicodemus had taken a pledge in front of witnesses to spend his whole life observing the scribal law in all its detail. Since that time his life had centred around the law. In the synagogue he had spent his days studying and expounding the law. It had been his belief that from its great, wide principles could be drawn rules and regulations to cover every situation life might present. To draw out these rules and to regulate his living accordingly had been his constant aim. In this way what had begun as life had ended as legalism. Nicodemus had become, like all his party, obsessed with the trivial, life at ground level.

He fell upon the nocturnal haunt of Jesus. His opener was already prepared. The line of his theoretical argument –

which might enlist the support of Jesus for the reforming party – had been thought through in advance.

But Jesus ignored his compliment, homed in on his need – and, in the conversation that ensued, laid an axe at the root of the whole system Nicodemus represented.

'Except a man be born again, he cannot see the kingdom of God.'[1]

Nicodemus was great on *theory*. But in the area of first principles had not even mastered the alphabet.

Jesus told him what was needed. Not a *reformed* man, but a *transformed* man. Not a new leaf, but a new *life*. Not a life of barren legalism – the righteousness of the Pharisees – but a life rebuilt through the power of God.

'Ye must be born again.'[2]

Chop-fallen, on the defensive, Nicodemus resorted to sarcasm:

'How can a man be born when he is old?'[3]

His tone was spiked with bitterness. He was stung by the thought of a kingdom too pure for a Pharisee to enter. Hurt by the implication that the way to salvation was along quite another road than that which had worn his feet to the bone.

But the question Nicodemus asked of Jesus did not query the *desirability* of the new birth, merely its *possibility*.

A compulsion had brought Nicodemus to Jesus. That compulsion was born of the fact that his feet *were* worn to the bone on the road of legalism. He was right up against the eternal problem: the problem of a man who wants to be changed and who cannot change himself.

Jesus had seen the dilemma from the outset and had come right in with the answer. Nicodemus needed rebuilding from scratch by the Master Builder. Needed to have the motive of law-keeping as a means to salvation replaced by the response of love to the work of the Master Builder. Needed to be reborn to 'a lively hope'.[4]

But Nicodemus was shaking his head, saying, 'How can these things be?'[5]

Jesus began to talk about things that Nicodemus knew about. He reminded him of the plague of serpents in the history of ancient Israel. At that time healing had only come to those who had looked up at the symbolic form of a serpent uplifted by Moses on a banner staff (a cross). They had been saved, Jesus was saying, not by fastidious attention to any law, but by looking – to the Saviour foreshadowed by the banner staff.

Look, believe – and be saved! This was the message of Jesus to Nicodemus. In the words that followed He expressed His Gospel neatly in a few words:

'For God so loved the world, that he gave his only begotten Son, that whosoever believeth in him should not perish, but have everlasting life.'[6]

This has been called the greatest verse in Scripture. Why? Because it concerns the greatest Giver: God. Because it mentions the greatest thing in the world: love. Because it refers to the greatest group it is possible to love: the world. Because it mentions the greatest evidence of love: giving. Because it enshrines the greatest gift ever bestowed: the only begotten Son of God. Because it includes the greatest invitation: whosoever. Because the only condition mentioned is one of the greatest simplicity: believing. Because it concerns avoiding the greatest fate: perishing. Because it promises the greatest of rewards: eternal life.

These words are chock-full with significant truth. They tell us that the world is not an iceberg but a ship, that its Captain is God, who is love. It affirms that man has become bad and needs changing. It warns that a judgement day is coming, and only those found in Christ will survive that day. It promises that this world will not always live under the spectral shadow of death, disease, famine and misery, sin-cursed, but that all shadows will disappear in the everlasting Light of everlasting life. And more yet – it sets forth simply the 'how' of salvation – 'That whosoever believeth in Him'.

By believing on the Lord Jesus Christ the sinner's *guilt* is removed. He is justified.

By believing on the Lord Jesus Christ and looking to Him the *power* of sin is on the wane in the believer's experience. He is *sanctified*. The rebel, having laid down his weapons, has sided with the right.

Through believing in Him, at length the Christian comes to

meet the Master again – when He returns in glory. Then the very *presence* of sin is removed. And with his Saviour he is *glorified*.

Under Jerusalem's night sky Nicodemus had been privileged to hear 'the Bible in miniature'. The words from the mouth of Jesus have thrilled Christians down through the ages. Martin Luther's understanding of these words enabled him to understand the writings of Paul correctly. When he launched the great Reformation he inserted the word *'sola'*, that is *'alone'*, into Romans 3:28, giving the true meaning of the verse by rendering it: 'Therefore we conclude that a man is justified by faith *alone* without the deeds of the law.'

Everything hinged on believing. So what is believing? The gospel of John is dedicated to answering that question. Believing is 'seeing', according to John 3:11; it is 'coming', according to John 6:35; it is 'receiving', according to John 1:12. Believing is getting right out of oneself and getting right into Christ. It is taking Him into account in everything – what He is, what He has done, what He is doing, and what He has promised yet to do. It is making Christ to the mind and heart what food is to the body.

'Ye must be born again', Nicodemus had heard Jesus say. When a man is born again he makes a 180-degree turn. What was formerly ahead of him becomes behind him. What was formerly behind him is ahead of him. Good and evil change places. With his eyes on the Saviour he is walking in a new direction, embarked upon a new adventure.

The truth dawned on Nicodemus. Whether one was a Sadducee or a Pharisee mattered nothing. Whether one was a Jew or a Gentile mattered nothing. 'Whosoever believeth on Him' was all.

'He that believeth on him is not condemned: but he that believeth not is condemned already.'[7] He is condemned because he has refused the gift of grace. Jesus concluded: 'And this is the condemnation, that light is come into the world, and men loved darkness rather than light.'[8]

* * *

As Nicodemus retraced his steps through the olive groves

to the Golden Gate his mind was in turmoil. He was turning from the 'light' and was going back to the 'darkness' of dead religion. But the light of Jesus burned within him.

As the months and years passed by he endeavoured on many occasions to exert a moderating influence upon the Sanhedrin. But the great change came, the fire consumed him, he was *born again*, when he saw the Saviour 'lifted up' on the central cross on Skull Hill. Looking into the pain-drawn, blood-stained face of the One he had once encountered in the firelight of a clearing in the Mount of Olives, he knew what had to be done.

1 John 3:3. **2** John 3:7. **3** John 3:4. **4** 1 Peter 1:3. **5** John 3:9. **6** John 3:16. **7** John 3:18. **8** John 3:19.

NORTH INTO GALILEE

12

Here was another world. A world apart from what we had left behind that morning, jangling and noisome, its hard, bitter passions somehow summed up in the word Judea.

As we sat by the quayside it seemed that here, by Galilee, was a land of neither night nor day, but a rouged, perpetual twilight. In from the further shore, across the flat, crimson silence, a little fleet came throbbing to land.

From our table at a water's-edge restaurant we awaited dinner. Below us the dark waters of Galilee were teeming with fish. A few yards away on a slender strip of beach, gauzy with nets, the fishermen were drawing their catch wallowing ashore.

Fish figured prominently on the menu. We had ordered 'St. Peter's Fish' and now, waiting, hoped that our vegetarian sensibilities would not be too outraged.

We were served a large, whole, cooked fish with fins, tail, head – and an eye staring accusingly. We covered it with the half lemon. If we *had* to eat him he need not be a witness to the deed.

Lights twinkled from the communities around the lake and an army of scrawny cats slunk in an out from under the tables, hoping that we would leave some of our entrée. We did not disappoint them.

Listening to the sob of the brimming water of the Sea of Galilee that *other* world from which we had driven in the course of the day was losing its reality.

* * *

Over dinner at Jerusalem the previous evening the conversation had been intense. There had been massacres in Beirut. It was generally believed that the Phalange had committed them with the connivance of the Israeli army and government. A commission of enquiry which would report twelve months hence would substantiate this assumption;

cabinet resignations would result. But, in our group, the worst had anyway been assumed.

Atrocities committed against Palestinians in Lebanon – at this time, because of the Israeli invasion, a microcosmic replica of the twisted perplexities of the Middle East power game – juddered a violent reaction throughout Israel's Palestinian population. An explosion of anti-Israeli bitterness and sheer frustration could be expected imminently.

'Pity anyone who is travelling through West Bank territories tomorrow!' said a student of politics from the Hebrew university.

We were.

We asked for advice.

If we took the Jordan route, we were told, we would be stoned. If we took the route through the mountains of Samaria we could expect violence in Ramallah or Nablus.

In the event we had taken the latter route.

We had encountered hostile stares, harsh words, some spitting and, in the towns, the grim determination of pedestrians and donkey and camel drivers not to allow cars through until they were good and ready.

The newspapers for the day would report violence in all the towns through which we passed. But we did not see it. Nevertheless, there were under-the-surface rumblings that seemed to be building up to an eruption of Krakatoan proportions.

At no point between Jerusalem and Tiberias was it possible to stop the car.

We drove close by Bethel, but were forced grimly to pass on. Jacob's well near Nablus was closed up; men with machine guns were everywhere, and not all of them were Israeli soldiers.

The ruins of ancient Shiloh, once the religious centre of the tribes of Israel, were seen at a distance – but we powered on by.

Sebaste (old Samaria), Ahab's capital, had to remain unvisited.

We drove as slowly as we dared through the mountain passes of Samaria. Up in the hills the day was quiet and golden. And there was a broad, verdant beauty which made

Jerusalem and its surrounding terrain seem desolate by comparison.

Down in the valleys we heard explosions. The sound rolled round and over the hills. But we saw nothing.

Mid-afternoon we descended on Tiberias. As we dropped below sea level on the mountain road from the north-west the heavy heat enveloped us. In the distance were the oil-blue waters of Galilee, innocent in the naked sun.

Tiberias, we found, was a curious place. Amid ruins of Crusader castles and the rubble left by Jordanian guns, Tiberias had grown a rash of ill-constructed, higgledy-piggledy clubs and discos – all run by far-from-orthodox Jews. Towering above were great concrete monoliths, soon to become hotels and 'holiday homes', an earnest of the Israeli intention to make this town into a wind-surfing, speed-boating, sun-soaking Benidorm-by-Galilee.

But vulgarity is nothing new to Tiberias. Earlier in the century H. V. Morton found 'jumbled shops' and the narrow streets of a squalid shanty town mixed up with Herodian ruins, and the broken fragments of a Crusader wall of black basalt.[1]

In the early childhood of Jesus Galilee contained only one city, Sepphoris, five miles from Nazareth. But, following the accession of the Emperor Tiberius in AD 14, Herod Antipas began to build a new capital on Galilee. It was completed in AD 22. Its magnificent excesses would be a subject of discussion in the carpenter's workshop at Nazareth. In these years even the smallest towns of Galilee contained some 15,000 inhabitants.[2] At one time the population of Sepphoris had been comparable to that of Jerusalem.[3] And Herod's sprawl at Tiberias, we may be sure, would be built to outdo Sepphoris.

Poking around modern Tiberias for Herodian remains today, however, is an overrated pastime. Of the Roman pleasure villas which lined the amethyst-green shore, there is nothing. Herod constructed many of his buildings of white marble; but Roman coins, pottery and tiny fragments of iridescent glass are all that you are likely to find these days.

On the first full day in Tiberias we set out in search of the palace of Antipas. During the ministry of Jesus it stood upon the acropolis, arising out of the black basalt cliffs of the mountainside, dominating the whole shoreline as a grim symbol of military might and kingly power. We did find the hill – above the tombs of the rabbis. But the rubble there was twentieth, not first century, and was there courtesy of the guns of King Hussein of Jordan, not the builders of Herod, tetrarch of Galilee.

When constructing this city Herod's builders had disturbed a vast cemetery. They had built over it and, before the dirt was packed hard between the stones of its streets, the rabbis had declared the city unclean. Antipas had, in consequence, to import the poor of other towns to populate his gleaming new city.

Galilee means 'Ring of the Gentiles'. Ten cities of Galilee were given by Solomon to the King of Tyre as part-payment for building materials used in the construction of the Temple. The influx of the Gentiles had continued in later centuries. In the towns and villages around the western shore where Jesus preached, the non-Jewish element was very strong.[4]

'Thou art a Galilean', said a Jewish house-servant to Peter on the night of Jesus' arrest.[5] And he was affronted. Galileans were stereotyped as broad-skulled peasantry, with guttural speech and absurd grammar. But idealism reigned in Galilee. And that idealism expressed itself in patriotism, and an openness of mind which Galileans did not encounter on their thrice-yearly sojourns in Jerusalem.

As for Tiberias, it is only mentioned once in the gospels, and there is no evidence that Jesus preached there or, indeed, went there. Only the hot, mineral springs, where the Romans bathed, remain as an authentic relic.

* * *

As we perched on the rubble where the palace of Antipas once stood, we thought of that dynasty whose paranoid kings, from their cameo parts, provide a chill of menace to the four gospels.

Jesus was born in the last year of Herod the Great. To some he appeared the enlightened ruler. Beyond comparison, he was the great builder. There was the Temple, the Antonia

Fortress, his own palace, the walls and so much more – in Jerusalem. He had built Caesarea on the coast, the vaunted table-mountain city of Masada, and the fortified palace near Bethlehem, Herodion.

The influence of Hellenistic culture was strong upon him, religion to be valued as 'a social cement'. Thus he erected temples to the godhead of Caesar at Sebaste, Phoenicia, Tyre and Caesarea Philippi. He renewed the Pythian temple at Rhodes. He ingratiated himself with the Idumaeans – from whom his own family came – by building them sanctuaries at Mamre. In Hebron he pandered to the cult of Abraham by building the edifice of Machpelah.

But, the veneer peeled off, the Hellenistic sophisticate was as ruthless as the most barbarous eastern despot. Tricked by the wise men from the east he 'sent forth, and slew all the children that were in Bethlehem',[6] a hideous act, but one which was of a piece with the rest of his life. A paranoia which has few equals in history led him to murder – by strangling, stabbing and poison – his closest relations, including his wife Mariamne and her two sons. In the last days of his life, a mass of disease and insanity, he ordered the execution of his natural successor, his son Antipater. He built the great Temple on Mount Moriah, but the whole nation prayed for him to die.

Three sons succeeded him.

Archelaus inherited Samaria, Ituria and the Kingdom of Judea. Debauched and degenerate, he had the primeval brutality of his father, but none of his topsoil urbanity. Mary and Joseph, with the child Jesus, had been exiled in Egypt to avoid the excesses of Herod the Great. On the old king's death Joseph decided that it was safe to return. 'But when he heard that Archelaus was reigning in Judea in place of his father Herod, he was afraid to go there. Having been warned in a dream, he withdrew to the district of Galilee, and he went and lived in a town called Nazareth.'[7] Eventually, because of his excesses, Herod the Great's eldest surviving son was summoned to Rome to appear before Caesar. Providing no satisfactory answer to a long list of his misdeeds he was banished to Gaul. At the time of this banishment Jesus was a

The Western Wall, once the Wailing Wall, so sacred to Jews. The lower section formed part of the supporting walls bounding the outer court of the temple at the time of Jesus. Inset right: The Wall assumes particular significance on the anniversary of the creation of the State of Israel.

Above: The synagogue of Capernaum which recent discoveries by archaeologists have linked with the time of Jesus. Below: The Jordan Valley from Jericho.

child of ten. The territories of Archelaus were now to be ruled by the Sanhedrin under the control of a governor appointed by Rome with his headquarters at Caesarea. From AD 26-36 the governor was called Lucius Pontius Pilate.

Antipas, Herod's second son, became tetrarch of Galilee and Peraea. He acquired a reputation for deviousness rather than brutality. This reputation led Jesus to describe him as 'that fox'.[8] He contracted an incestuous marriage with his brother's wife, Herodias. In addition to building Tiberias he also reconstructed a fortress at Machaerus, on the barren heights of Moab above the Dead Sea. There he lived with Herodias and her daughter Salome. It is not clear whether John the Baptist's fulmination against the match was at Tiberias or Machaerus. However, it is believed that John's decapitation, at the behest of Herodias, took place at Machaerus. But it was in the Herodian palace at Jerusalem, near the site of the present-day Jaffa Gate, that Antipas played his part in the trial of Jesus.

Herod the Great's third son, Philip, became tetrarch of the remote region north of Galilee, centring around Caesarea Philippi and in the vicinity of the modern Golan Heights.

The Herod who participated in Christ's trial and must take responsibility for the death of John the Baptist, Antipas, was himself to have a sad end. He had harboured his wife's brother, Agrippa. Agrippa was an adventurer with a warped mind and no conception of loyalty. He ingratiated himself with the mad emperor Caligula. Caligula gave him the title of king and assigned him the territories of Antipas and of Philip the tetrarch. Antipas and Herodias, their palaces and possessions handed over to Agrippa, ended their lives in disgrace in Gaul.

* * *

But while Jerusalem is evocative of Pilate and Peter, Caiaphas and Christ, and the thorn-cruel world of the first century seems close at hand, Tiberias has lost even the faintest glimmer of the memory of Antipas and Herodias. The guide books are encumbered with the names of long-dead rabbis, but the long-dead founder of the city finds no men-tion. Tiberias bears him no memorial.

* * *

Our days spent there were spacious, slow and quiet. They moved timeless, unsorted, gliding gently into one another.

Then one morning, golden with inevitable sun, we awoke to the singing of a melodious female voice. It had a beautiful timbre, soft and modulated.

We watched on the balcony as she sang to the calm, blue water. Her features were a curious mixture of Greek and Hebrew lines, an almost stencilled perfection. Her hair was as red as the copper dug from the mines of Cyprus and burnished in the forges of Paphos.

We thought of another Jewish beauty who, in another age, sang her song to that city. But found in its echoes only depravity and disappointment. Until, that is, she met another Singer and learned another Song. . . .

1 H. V. Morton, *In the Steps of the Master*, page 183. **2** Josephus Flavius, *The Jewish War*, vol. 3, pages 42-44. **3** John Wilkinson, *Jerusalem as Jesus Knew It: Archaeology as Evidence*, page 23. **4** H. V. Morton, op cit, page 175. **5** Mark 14:70. **6** Matthew 2:16. **7** Matthew 2:19-23, NIV. **8** Luke 13:32.

IN SEARCH OF MARY OF MAGDALA

13

They would have called Mary of Magdala *meretrix*, prostitute.

Such women were common in every garrison town. The presence of the vast establishment of Herod Antipas would have ensured that there would be quite a number around the narrow streets and jetties of Tiberias.

Magdala (Migdal) is only two miles down the road from Tiberias. Its squat dwellings cower under the sinister Horns of Hittin, two menacing mountain peaks separated by a ravine. Here Saladin won his decisive victory over the Crusaders. Through the ravine at the time of Christ passed the great east-west road.

Magdala was a small town a little inland from Galilee but very much involved in the fishing industry – specifically, drying and salting – and rendered just a little more cosmopolitan than some of the lakeside towns because of her contact with the traders on the Great Road, and just a little less innocent – because of her enforced contact with her near neighbour, Tiberias.

In Tiberias they demanded entertainment. And, while dark-faced Nabatean musicians from the desertlands of the south played their reed-pipes and resonant scabella, a Jewish girl might earn a little money singing in the streets. Only to find that when the rosiness had died out of the sunset Tiberias had taken on a different character and the shouts from the men who lined the waterfront had become suggestive, then demanding.

Roman courtesans wielded a powerful influence upon their admirers and enjoyed a certain status in Roman-colonial society. But not so among the Jews. There was but one word for the women of their conquerors, whether wives, daughters, mistresses or even street singers. The word was 'Jezebel'. And, walking the two miles home to Magdala, the moon-path broad on the water before her, Mary would have learned to wince at its lash, eyes bubbling for lost innocence.

But many authorities – including at least one time-tested classic on the life of Christ – would have Mary weeping for an innocence lost long before she had come into contact with the depravities of Tiberias. Before even, she *was* 'Mary of Magdala'.[1]

There are powerful reasons for believing that Mary of Bethany and Mary of Magdala were the same person. Among these would be the sheer importance of 'Mary Magdalene' in the gospel story. Then there would be the close relationship of Jesus with the Bethany family. But perhaps most conclusively the fact that the fallen woman present at the feast of Simon the Pharisee in Bethany is specifically identified in the fourth gospel as Mary, sister of Martha and Lazarus.[2]

The identification of the two Marys as one demands explanation and leads to a fascinating reconstruction of Mary's story.

This reconstruction requires that Mary's fall took place in Bethany, not Tiberias, and was occasioned, not by a Roman soldier or a depraved Herodian courtier, but by 'a citizen above reproach'.

* * *

Jesus had no home to call His own. His 'family' had become the motley crew of disciples who shared His life-style – the gentle dreamer, John; the practical tax collector, Levi Matthew; the weak, but headstrong fisherman, Peter; the quizzical Thomas; seafaring men of the ilk of Andrew and James; plus a handful of others.

But there was one home in which He was always welcome. It was in Bethany, on the eastern slopes of the Mount of Olives. It was tenanted by Lazarus and his sisters, Mary and Martha. Lazarus was the breadwinner, their parents apparently being dead. Mary would be an apple-cheeked, outgoing girl; the life and soul of every social function. Martha, to the contrary, would appear to have been perpetually in a dither of anxiety with a head bursting with kitchen-sink concerns; very much a home-spun character. But Martha, too, was in demand at social functions: to do the catering.

In Bethany there also lived one of Jerusalem's most prominent Pharisees, Simon. He fitted well into the characterization of Pharisees in Jesus' stern denunciation.[3] Hypocrisy was an essential ingredient of Simon's legalistic religion; he would 'strain out a gnat but swallow a camel'.[4] Nicodemus the Pharisee had been seeking for truth. Simon the Pharisee was a spiritual schizophrenic.

Simon presumably met Mary socially and decided he wanted to get to know her better. Nicodemus might have said: 'Get thee behind me Satan, and don't push!' But Simon didn't. He mulled the thought over. Mary suspected nothing; she was used to being well liked. One thing led to another and Simon, the citizen above reproach, led Mary into sin.

But Simon had his position to think about. Soon he would be using his ecclesiastical leverage to lever Mary out of town. And Mary would require very little levering.

The word would soon get around in Bethany. 'Have you heard about Mary?'

One day Mary would leave Bethany with no 'goodbyes'. Perhaps she took the road down into Jericho, and then followed the Jordan north to Galilee, passing through Tiberias before settling in the small town which cowered under the stark Arvel cliffs. Magdala.

In Magdala perhaps Mary wanted nothing more than to leave the past behind. But reputations have a habit of overtaking as we run. Perhaps Mary began to get hungry and discouraged. . . . How was she to acquire some easy money?

Tiberias was just two miles down the road. She would have seen the street singers as she passed through. Perhaps she joined them, and found the after-dark suggestions difficult to resist. Perhaps, in Tiberias, Mary found her easy money.

The name of Mary of Magdala became widely known. She amassed a small fortune. Later in the story we find her with an alabaster box of the most expensive perfumed ointment it was possible to buy. Did she buy it from one of the merchants on the Great Road that passed by Magdala – as an investment?

Inside Mary there was a vast chasm of despair.

At one point in His Galilean ministry Jesus 'took ship, and came into the coasts of Magdala'.[5] Perhaps it was then that Mary first met Him. If it was, then Mary would have heard the Pharisees and the Sadducees taunt Him and would have been amazed to have heard Jesus call them 'a wicked and adulterous generation'.[6]

But as well as words of denunciation which exposed the hypocrisy of the religious leaders, there were words of hope for sinners. Sin He hated; sinners, apparently, He loved. Jesus did not simply tolerate them, 'holding His nose while He treated their moral wounds'.[7] He was no professional 'do-gooder'. He accepted sinners and they were glad to accept Him.

Perhaps she heard the Pharisees say: 'This man receiveth sinners.'[8] The words were said sneeringly, but to Mary they would be the words of resurrection and life uttered over the grave of all her hopes.

Over the heads of the crowd streaming into Magdala perhaps Mary caught snatches of what the travelling preacher was saying.

'Come unto me all ye that labour and are heavy laden and I will give ye rest.'

'He that cometh unto me I will in no wise cast out.'

Mary's heart began to punch a gap through her rib cage. *This Man receiveth sinners!*

The devil would do his best: 'That doesn't mean you, Mary. You've gone too far. You are an outcast.'

But Jesus said: *'He that cometh unto me I will in no way cast out.'*

Anyone, any time, anywhere, who sincerely comes to Jesus is always, always accepted.

So in the press and throng of Magdala, Mary was 'converted'. What is *conversion?* It is a supernatural work of the Holy Spirit on the human heart. It is being turned around to walk in a new direction.

But conversion was not the end of the road for Mary, only the beginning. Many times she fell down on the road.

Jesus went on His way and, it would appear, Mary made the mistake of staying on in Magdala. The same voices whispered over her shoulder. The same figures came to her door. She had sat at the feet of Jesus – been pardoned of her sin – but had not learned how to sit at the feet of Jesus when Jesus was not in town.

Again Mary was pardoned.

Again Mary fell.

At least *seven times* Jesus cast devils out of Mary.[9]

Then Mary learned how to sit at the feet of Jesus when Jesus was not in town. Mary learned, not only forgiveness of sin, but how to live the Christian life. She learned what the apostle Paul was to express so neatly: 'By grace are ye saved through faith; and that not of yourselves: it is the gift of God: not of works, lest any man should boast.'[10] Mary learned that she could not *work* her passage to the Kingdom of God; could not become righteous by dint of hard slog, her own exertions. Only by the power of faith that Jesus provides. She learned also that she could only receive this power by looking to Him, by staying close to Him every day of her life – whether He was in town or not!

Mary began to experience victories over sin. She even screwed up the courage to return to Bethany. With her she took that expensive alabaster box of perfume.

When she arrived at the outskirts of the village she heard the hollow sound of a leper's 'Unclean! Unclean!' There was a familiar inflexion in the voice. It was Simon. Driven out from his position at the synagogue he was reduced to announcing his contagion and begging for crumbs.

Mary hurried by to the open arms of Martha and Lazarus.

Bethany adjusted to Mary. She lived with her past, knowing that God had forgiven and forgotten it. When Jesus came up from Jericho with His disciples one day, it was natural that He should call and visit Mary and Martha, equally natural that Mary should sit at His feet, and very typical that Martha should be 'cumbered about with much caring' and elicit the mild reproof from Jesus.[11] Respectable as she was, Martha also needed Jesus, and if she was too busy to spend time sitting at His feet she was too busy.

It was not long after this incident that Mary and Martha needed all the faith they could muster. Lazarus became seriously ill. Jesus was sent for. But He did not arrive until four days after Lazarus had died. Martha showed irritation; but at the same time great faith. 'I believe', she said, 'that thou art the Christ, the Son of God.' Practical, aproned souls can learn to sit at the feet of Jesus too. Outside the rock-hewn tomb Jesus pronounced the words: *'Lazarus, come forth.'*[12]

The next time Jesus entered Bethany by the Jericho Road, He, like Mary, heard the cry, 'Unclean'. And Jesus could not leave a man suffering by the side of the road – even if he did richly deserve to suffer. Jesus touched the untouchable and made him whole.

However, though expelled from the synagogue because of his condition, Simon was at base still a Pharisee. And Pharisees were used to *earning* what they received. It may have been in an effort to repay Jesus for His miraculous act of healing that Simon organized a feast in His honour.

Everyone was there. Except Mary. Her presence Simon would not tolerate. 'Martha served.'[13] She would also appear to have let Mary in by a back entrance. Mary was not a wallflower by nature and, in any event, she had heard Jesus say that He would be betrayed into the hands of sinful men and put to death. This might be her last opportunity to see Him. She had a gift for Him. Something special.

She had planned to deliver her gift quietly and then leave. The olive lamps would be burning low and she could creep through the shadows. No one would know.

No one did know – until she opened the alabaster box of ointment. The perfume permeated the room; then *everyone* knew. Covered with confusion she anointed the feet of Jesus with the ointment and dried them with her hair. As Mary scurried away Jesus said, 'Let her alone.'

At the top of the table Simon was thinking, 'If this Man were really a prophet He would know what sort of woman this is.'

Jesus read his thoughts.

Without embarrassing Simon in public Jesus told a story that only Simon would understand. It told Simon that Jesus could see right through him. It broke his heart. Jesus accepted that broken heart. Simon was converted.

'This Man receiveth sinners', they had said. And without knowing it they had expressed the central truth of the Christian Gospel. Jesus received Mary and Martha and Lazarus and Simon the Pharisee.

* * *

In modern Migdal, set in an area of lush agricultural land between the Horns of Hittin and the Sea of Galilee, they still remember Mary. They remember her, too, in Bethany for, as Jesus said, 'Wheresoever this gospel shall be preached in the whole world, there shall also this, that this woman hath done, be told for a memorial of her.'[14] But more than anywhere else she is remembered at the entrance of an empty tomb which she was the first to discover.

1 E. G. White, *The Desire of Ages*. See especially pages 566-568; M. Venden, *Salvation by Faith and Your Will*, pages 111-128. These sources are used as the basis for this chapter's reconstruction of Mary's story. **2** Matthew 26:6-13; Mark 14:3-11; Luke 7:36-50; John 12:1-9. **3** Matthew 23. **4** Matthew 23:24, NIV. **5** Matthew 15:39. **6** Matthew 16:1, 4. **7** F. F. Bruce, *The Real Jesus*, page 46. **8** Luke 15:2. **9** Mark 16:9; E. G. White, op cit, page 568. **10** Ephesians 2:8, 9. **11** Luke 10:38-42. **12** John 11:1-45. **13** John 12:2, NIV. **14** Matthew 26:13.

TWO MOUNTAINS

14

The dry, hot wind from the east was blowing as we headed for Sinai. An ancient prophet had called it 'a scorching wind from the high bare places in the wilderness'.[1]

It was full of whirling sand, tearing at the eyes, working into the mouth, worming under doors and wriggling through shutters.

The simoom wind some called it. Nerves were taut, tempers barely in rein. In the kibbutzim in the Negev they told us that, if a man murdered his wife when the desert wind was blowing, the court would be likely to acquit him.

Our lips were swollen, our throats parched with an imperious thirst. When Jesus lived a man caught on a journey by the hot wind could only wrap his head in his burnous, turn his back on the wind and wait – while swirling sand filled his nostrils and his throat.

We dreamt of air conditioning and cool water.

But the wind did not reach up into Sinai. Here the air was breathable, though the sky was still burning.

Mount Sinai; a triangle of mountains, a rock barrier between Asia and Africa. From the summit, 2,260 metres above sea level, we looked over a wild vision of gaunt ridges and cragged peaks exuding the breath of the Old Testament. Here God gave His stone-written record of ten eternal principles which were to be the sub-structure of justice, right, duty, privilege, security. A sub-structure itself built, as Jesus pointed out,[2] on a foundation of love.

* * *

You could cross the planet and not have a sharper contrast than that which exists between Sinai and Galilee. In Galilee 200 metres below sea level, the air was humid, not dry. The contours were gentle, the lap of the wavelets soothing to frayed nerves. And everywhere there was colour.

Desert nights on the foothills of Sinai had been cold. Galilean nights seemed as hot and humid as Galilean days. In the monastery on Sinai there had been a problem keeping warm. In the Church of Scotland Centre in Tiberias the nights posed the opposite problem.

Galilean night-heat was heavy and seemed to close us in. The 'helicopter' fan whirred noisily and rocked dangerously just below the ceiling, but brought not a breath of coolth. We crunched on chunks of ice from the fridge. Sleep was impossible.

The buildings of the Church of Scotland Centre were constructed a century ago as a hospital. Now they serve as a hospice for pilgrims. The narrow, high arches of the veranda reminded us of a Victorian colonial governor's residence.

Respite from the heat by day could only be had by travelling above the 400 metre mountain wall which fronts Galilee to the west. The most beautiful of the mountains is the Mount of the Beatitudes whose gentle slopes rise to the north-west of the lake. Breath-snatching views are to be had through the arches of the veranda that completely surrounds the beautiful, octagonal church built to commemorate the Sermon on the Mount, believed to have been preached from these slopes.

The inland sea – unpolluted, the main reservoir of fresh water in Israel – because of the heat haze, had a dreamy quality about it. The shore-line was green and soft, there were vines and banana groves. To the north, set back, beyond a lush green valley rising from the shore, set against the eternal azure, were the violet mountains of Golan and the snow-capped peak of Mount Hermon.

What a setting for a sermon!

The ministry of Jesus had begun with His baptism in the Jordan.

The forty days in the Judean wilderness had been a preparation time.

The action was about to begin.

But before a man sets his hand to a great crusade he needs helpers. Jesus chose twelve.

Before the helpers could be of practical use they required intensive instruction. Jesus preached the Sermon on the

Mount. It was the Magna Charta of the Kingdom, the Manifesto of the King. In it Jesus opened His mind to His disciples.

At first He spoke about joy. The Greek word was *makarios*. And *makarios* was a bedrock, indestructible joy. It was a joy not dependent on the chance of circumstances, and was far more than 'happiness'. It was a joy that no one could take away from the follower of Christ.[3] It shone through sorrow. It melted pain. It dried tears. And it was a joy of the here-and-now.

There was the joy of the man who knew he was helpless and must depend completely upon his Lord. The Kingdom of Heaven would be his.

There was the joy of the man who experienced heart-broken sorrow for the sufferings of the world – and for his own sin. He would find the joy of God.

There was the joy of the meek man – not the *timid* man, the *tamed* man; the man whose power was under control. *He* would inherit the earth, be a king among men.

There was the joy of a man who was famished for righteousness, who thirsted for it like one caught in the simoom wind of the desert thirsted for water. *He* would receive it.

There was the joy of a man who could walk in another man's moccasins, see with *his* eyes, feel with *his* feelings. Such a man would find that God would do likewise for him.

The joy of the man 'without side', who did things for the loftiest of reasons, who kept his heart clean. *He* was fitting himself some day to see God.

There was the joy of the man who not only said, 'Shalom' but practised it, *created* it in his relations with others. He was helping God with God's own work.

Then there was the joy of the persecuted; the joy of 'the panting, huddled flock whose only crime was Christ', the 'little flock', who down through the arches of the centuries would suffer for the name of Christ. Their reward would be great. It was His Father's good pleasure to give them the Kingdom.[4]

* * *

From His panegyric on joy Jesus went on to *Law*, the guts

of His sermon. Law, the link between Sinai and the Mount of the Beatitudes, the bridge between Old and New Testaments, God's eternal code of conduct.

The disciples would prick up their ears when Jesus mentioned Law. Their minds would be broadened, enlightened beyond the conventional religion of their day as Jesus explained the great principles of the Law in all their dimensions. 'The sermon on the mount takes up where the ten commandments leave off.'[5]

But the most startling statement of all would have been when He said:

'Do not think that I have come to abolish the Law or the Prophets; I have not come to abolish them but to fulfil them. I tell you the truth, until heaven and earth disappear, not the smallest letter, not the least stroke of a pen, will by any means disappear from the Law until everything is accomplished.'[6]

From the Galilean mount Jesus reached back to Sinai. On Sinai He had written the broad principles of right in stone. Now they were reiterated, amplified, confirmed. Not the crossing of a T nor the dotting of an I would be changed – 'until heaven and earth disappear'.

Is this where, like the disciples, *we* prick up *our* ears? Is this a message the modern world needs to take to its heart? Is it possible that many of the problems of *our* society have arisen because certain obligations imposed by God's loving but unaccommodating code have proved unpalatable to the jaded tastes of 'liberated man' – and have been set aside?

Since no one will dispute the contention that they *have* been set aside, dare we examine the consequences?

Every character in every plot, every situation in every scene, every line of the entire script of this great Play for Today is stained with the weeping poison of that characteristically modern viewpoint that guilt is to be healed by lowering standards, *that we need no law*. Personality problems, home problems, marriage problems and juvenile problems, violence in the classrooms, on the streets, in the tower blocks, on the terraces and in the living rooms, any and every social problem of this Play for Today in which *we* are actors shouts out the bankruptcy of that life-view that has sought to break down law and authority. And most importantly the divine Authority of God's Law.

To the 'modern theologian' who has to accept his share of the blame it must be said: To reject Jesus Christ at Sinai is to reject Him at the cross.

'Jesus Christ is the same yesterday, today, and for ever';[7] He was on Sinai, He preached on the Mount of the Beatitudes, and He was at Calvary – one and the same, ever One God.

The God of Sinai was at Calvary because the Law He had given man on Sinai was as changeless as His character, for it was an expression of it; and because that changeless Law had been broken. Sin had challenged God's Law and, because that Law must stand or the universe must fall, because the Law represents the foundation principles of right which cannot be set aside, the Son of God came to accept man's blame and die man's death – on Calvary.

'For sin pays its wage – death',[8] 'sin is a breaking of the law',[9] and God's love for man, as changeless as His law, made Him send His only Son to die because of man's transgression, that he might have the choice of eternal life, as opposed to the eternal death that would otherwise have been his lot.[10]

That is the meaning of Calvary.

If sin were nothing more than a personality deficiency and man a product of his environment and the arrangement of chromosomes, Calvary would not have been necessary.

God's stone-written record of ten eternal principles was considered 'holy, and just, and good' by Paul,[11] 'the Law of liberty' by James[12] and claimed as His own by Jesus who said, ' "If you love me, you will obey *my* commandments." '[13]

The Law does not save us, Calvary does. 'No-one will be declared righteous in his sight by observing the law; rather, through the law we become conscious of sin.'[14] Law is a mirror that reveals our imperfections,[15] but cannot correct them any more than a bathroom mirror can alter our face.

Law leads us to place our hand in the hand of the Man who, in blood, can write 'pardon' over our record.[16]

We are saved by grace through faith in Jesus Christ; and faith is a gift of God.[17]

What was 'nailed to the cross' was the collective weight of our sin.

When we see God's love and man's hate unveiled on Calvary, when we comprehend that Christ died in our place we are filled with wonder and our hearts are overcome with love. That love is more than sentiment; it has its outworking in our experience through obedience to God's Law. We keep the Law not *in order* to be saved, but because *we are* saved. The pardon we receive through Calvary does not give us licence to break God's Law, it only deepens our obligation to it.[18] The only Law 'done away with' at Calvary concerned the system of sacrifices that pointed forward to, and was fulfilled in, the cross.

On Sinai the stone-written principles of life and righteousness were given. On the Galilean mount Jesus reiterated that these principles should stand as long as time would last. But through His death and resurrection He unleashed the power upon the world which alone can lead us to victorious obedience.

* * *

'And it came to pass, when Jesus had ended these sayings, the people were astonished at his doctrine: for he taught them as one having authority and not as the scribes.'[19]

1 Jeremiah 4:11, NEB. **2** Matthew 22:35-40. **3** John 16:22. **4** This is a paraphrase of the Beatitudes (Matthew 5:3-12) using the original Greek text. See W. Barclay, *Gospel of Matthew*, vol. 1, pages 82-114. Jesus began the Sermon on the Mount (Matthew chapters 5, 6 and 7) with these affirmations. The Sermon on the Mount should be compared with the Sermon on the Plain in Luke 12:22-40. See especially verse 32. **5** F. F. Bruce, *The Real Jesus*, page 67. **6** Matthew 5:17, 18, NIV. **7** Hebrews 13:8, Good News Bible. **8** Romans 6:23, Good News Bible. **9** 1 John 3:4, Good News Bible. **10** John 3:16. **11** Romans 7:12. **12** James 2:12. **13** John 14:15, Good News Bible (italics ours). **14** Romans 3:20, NIV. **15** James 1:23-25. **16** Galatians 3:24. **17** Ephesians 2:8, 9. **18** Romans 6:14, 15. **19** Matthew 7:28, 29.

THE STREETS OF NAZARETH

15

There was a riot the day we went to Nazareth. A crowd of angry Palestinians went on the rampage, bitterness smarting in their eyes and venom spitting through clenched teeth.

The Arabs were caught in a poverty trap. Away from the main streets were the narrow alleyways where they lived, reminiscent of the Moslem Quarter in Old City Jerusalem. But poorer, fetid and decayed. Skinny wild cats, many with one eye and torn ears, darted from building to building over our feet. The young Arabs from the tumble-down dwellings had rallied to the PLO. Nazareth had a Communist mayor.

Away from the narrow streets and the smell of rotting refuse, we knew, was Upper Nazareth. Built in recent times for Ashkenazi Jews, it had four-lane, tree-shaded roads. In *old* Nazareth children were taught crammed into front rooms and flats. In Upper Nazareth there were uncrowded schools.

The Nazareth of the main streets was a big, busy, thundering town of industry and commerce. Heavy lorries struggled back and forth in roads throttled with cars and milling with coach-loads of tourists not at all sure where to go. There was the smell of petrol in the nose, the taste of dust in the mouth and the choke of exhaust fumes in the lungs.

We reluctantly abandoned our hire car amid a cluster of juddering, churning cement-mixers, and followed a crowd of German tourists. We turned into a narrow bazaar; refuse heaped in a gully down the middle of the pavement-wide street.

Above, hanging from sheets of corrugated iron, was an infinite variety of rubbish, some of it made in Hong Kong, selling for exorbitant prices. The *souk* was thronged with shoving, elbowing men and women of a score of nationalities. Never had we been so grateful that our valuables were safe in a body-belt.

After following a labyrinth of terraced alleys, climbing as we went, we entered a sun-bathed square. On two sides a red

Above: The Dome of the Rock, the Muslim mosque which dominates Temple Mount or Mount Moriah. In its cool interior is the sacred rock, the traditional site of Abraham's sacrificial altar. Below: The tranquil waters of the breath-takingly beautiful Sea of Galilee at sunset.

Above: The Lithostratos, the paving stones of the old Roman street outside the gates of the Antonia Fortress. Here a rabble once gathered to demand that Jesus be crucified. Below: The terraced slopes of the Mount of Olives.

tangle of bougainvillaea choked the trees and on another side was the gateway to the Church of the Annunciation.

Beyond the gateway was a huge basilica which, though modern, was beautiful in its simplicity. Built over a succession of architectural strata representing earlier edifices, in the lowest stratum was a cave. At either side of the entrance to the cave were two pillars going nowhere. Here, it is claimed, Mary received the announcement that she had been chosen from Israel's thousands to be mother of the longed-for Messiah.

Subdued tourists silently manoeuvred for a better view while an impressive mass was in progress and fifty or so of the devout knelt in worship. Oblivious to tourists and worshippers alike, a cleaning lady with bucket and mop made her way systematically over the floor. Angels might visit this spot from the realms of glory and the Holy Ghost might overshadow a virgin. Saladin, Richard Coeur de Lion and the Mameluke commanders might sacrifice thousands of lives in successive conquests of this spot. But to her it was just so many square yards of floor and, as such, to be cleaned and polished at the rate of so many shekelim an hour.

Across the way was the Church of St. Joseph, completed in the first years of the twentieth century. It was built over the ruins of earlier structures which inevitably, perhaps, were claimed to have been built over the original carpenter's shop.

We followed a party of Germans into the bowels of the building and examined the excavations. Most interesting was a full-sized baptistery where Christians, up to the tenth century, had practised baptism by immersion.

The carpenter's shop *may* have been in the electrically-lit cavern – topped by a conveniently placed grill through which tourists threw their coins down to what *may* have been the floor where Jesus learned and practised the trade of a tekton (carpenter/builder). But, as we returned to the car, we traversed another terraced street lined with the shops of artisans who worked in leather and in wood, and *here* we felt closer to the Master Carpenter whose yokes were easy, and whose burdens were light.

It was only as I watched an Arab wood-carver at work in

his miniscule workshop away from the arteries of tourism that the centuries sped away. Though, by standing in his doorway, I was blocking off a large part of his main source of light, he was oblivious to my presence. His fingers moved like lightning. Tools were taken up, deftly manipulated and put down. My imagination supplied the boy at his side, growing in wisdom and stature in favour with God and man. Then the sinewy Jesus of maturer years who heard in the winter winds blowing through the hill forest which supplied His timber, the wail of broken hearts calling that He might hasten to their relief, feeling at all times the pull of the great world of men whose souls He was on earth to save.

His Nazareth was a mere hamlet cradled in the hills of Galilee. For generations it had been the residence of descendants of the House of David. They called themselves *Natzoreans*, after the words of the prophet Isaiah (11:1): 'And there shall come forth a rod out of the stem of Jesse, and a Branch (or twig) shall grow out of his roots.' The Hebrew word for branch or twig was *netzer*. It was after this *netzer* that the village of Nazareth was named the Village of the Twig. Other descendants of David lived in nearby Kokhaba, Village of the Star.

Natzoreans lived in pious expectation of the Anointed One. But they must have puzzled over the prophecy that He should be born in Bethlehem[1] and of a virgin[2].

But a virgin from among the Natzoreans conceived. Having conceived she went south to the green, wooded hill country down mountain from Jerusalem. For at Ein Karem her cousin Elizabeth was expecting her own miracle child. And this miracle child would be forerunner to the Anointed One.

However, it took Caesar Augustus, architect of the Pax Romana, to bring Joseph and Mary, she in the last stages of her pregnancy, from Nazareth sixty miles south to Bethlehem.

Then it took Herod, the paranoiac Idumean, and the wiles of the Persian kings, to fulfil the prophecy of the Egyptian exile.[3] And Herod the Great's death to make it safe to return to Nazareth.

Hence it was in the hardscrabble environs of Nazareth that

He was reared. Not in a palace with an era's crown awaiting. Behind the bench of a tekton. Natzoreans might at one time have had a reputation for piety, but the Nazareth in which Jesus grew up had a bad one.[4]

No inbuilt advantage for the Son of God here. He was made 'in the likeness of sinful flesh', it being 'imperative that he should be made like his brothers in every respect', yet He 'knew no sin'.[5] 'God was in Christ, reconciling the world unto himself',[6] and to do so He had become part of His own creation, living down an ordinary street, making an ordinary living, having an ordinary education from an ordinary mother. But He had no ordinary character. Jesus was God-man, though His divinity was 'veiled', combined with human nature.

When Nazareth's tekton wanted new timber He could not select it from a wholesale timber yard. He shouldered His axe, not a chain saw, and made for the forested hills behind the town, where He had played as a boy. He selected His tree; and swung that axe. The wood must be hard. He would use it to make yokes, ploughs, benches, boats and houses.

There were no electric tools to help fashion the ox-yokes. Just a crude plane, a mallet and a chisel. The timber for benches had to be chipped with an adze until it was nicely smoothed.

'For you know the grace of our Lord Jesus Christ, that though he was rich, yet for your sakes he became poor, so that you through his poverty might become rich.'[7]

Rich in the inexhaustible resources for salvation in the eternal richness of the pre-existence of Christ who 'was in the beginning with God'.[8]

Poor, having taken on our infirmities, hunger, tiredness, sin-reduced capacities – but not our sin-broken relationship with God, having chosen to do the Father's will and being indwelt by the Spirit.[9]

* * *

The riot was in full howl as we approached the car. Shots were being fired, rocks were being thrown. And a young pickpocket was systematically making his way through the belongings of a crowd of tourists staring drop-jawed outside their luxury air-conditioned coach.

And Arab *pater-familias*, a spectator to the violence, asked if I was German. He liked Germans.

'Norr. Eez Eengleesh', said a younger companion and spat on the ground.

'That bad?' I enquired of the original questioner. But the home-baked crust of reserve that he wore like a breastplate did not shift.

Nudging the suddenly oh-so-fragile car past the now silent cement-mixers into the roar of the crowd, I wondered with the disciple, 'Can any good thing come out of Nazareth?'

1 Micah 5:2. **2** Isaiah 7:14. **3** Hosea 11:1. **4** John 1:46. **5** Romans 8:3; Hebrews 2:14-17, Phillips; 2 Corinthians 5:21. **6** 2 Corinthians 5:19. **7** 2 Corinthians 8:9, NIV. **8** John 1:1, 2. **9** Hebrews 10:7.

NAZARETH LOOKING BACK

16

Nazareth, even without a riot, would have been claustrophobic. We were amazed to emerge with the car intact.

Suddenly we caught a remarkable sight in the rear-view mirror. There was a town of snow-white houses, terraced on a hill. Fig and olive trees half covered each dwelling, with cypresses spearing above them.

Nazareth looked a great deal better from a distance.

Amid the jumble we could make out the old synagogue. We had hurried past it up the thronged *souk* on our way to more splendid places of worship. But looking back it seemed to stand out. The whole of the old town seemed to be configured around it.

The synagogue, whose dome is now topped by a cross, is owned by the Greek Orthodox Church. It has been the subject of controversy among historians and archaeologists. Most say that it dates from the sixth century. Certain it is that one Christian pilgrim visited it in AD 570. From his testimony one authority is prepared to believe that the synagogue is first century.

In whatever century it was built, the arrangement of the town and its archaeological remains strongly suggest that it was built over the site of earlier synagogues, including, doubtless, the one in which Jesus worshipped during the three silent Nazareth decades.

Here was, after all then, Nazareth's most authentic holy place.

All that was behind us. Ahead, as we took the road to Afula (Jezreel), was a steep downward slope, almost a precipice, with a road snaking beyond view to a plain hidden in heat mist.

Before we took on the twists and turns of the descending road we stopped for one last look at the turbulent town from which we had been so eager to escape.

From here its aspect was completely different. Behind it

were the wooded hills where Jesus played as a boy. There was the Virgin's Fountain, the only water supply from Nazareth until the present century. Mary would have carried water from this spring. It gushes out of the hillside, through a conduit to the fountain. The Greeks have built a church over its source.

Then we contemplated the view over the plain from the top of the steep scarp. In Christ's time it was the Plain of Esdraelon. In the Old Testament it was the Valley of Jezreel. The mists that covered it were like the ghosts of old armies. The boy Jesus well knew that this broad plain had thundered to the sound of many battles. Egypt, Assyria and Babylon had fought their battles there. There Barak had smashed the Canaanites. Here Gideon had driven the Midianites. Near the great Road to the Sea, Saul had consulted a witch at Endor. And, near the great Road to the Sea, seen his armies routed the following day.

Beyond the valley were the Hills of Samaria and, then, distant Carmel and the Great Sea, visible to the young Jesus when heat mists permitted. Elijah had stomped those hills, denouncing his king and calling down God's fire. These were the hills of Ahab and Jezebel. Months later we were to spend a day exploring them; visiting the Carmelite monastry on the headland above Haifa, and the 'high place' where the priests of Baal vainly called on their gods.

In Nazareth Jesus had lived above one of the great crossroads of the ancient world. Camel trains bore merchants along the road from Damascus to Egypt. He knew that Joseph had been sold down that road, to slavery. Alexander the Great had led his armies there, as Napoleon and Allenby would in later centuries. All travellers from all nations on all kinds of errands drove their camels on that road. And Jesus saw them.

If the road to Egypt was the Road to the South, the road from the sea was the Road to the East. Spices and silks weighed down the camel trains on that road. And Roman legions clanked their cumbersome way to the eastern frontier of the empire.

Signs of the rule of Rome were littered right across the

plain; marching soldiers, the ubiquitous tax collectors, rules of occupation nailed to tree trunks. And victims of occupation nailed to crosses. No fewer than 200,000 Jews lost their lives in futile rebellions in the century before the crucifixion; and how many of these Zealots, in the darkness, had swooped down on sleeping garrisons – from the hills behind Nazareth?

When Jesus was a boy of about 11 Judas the Galilean had led a rebellion against Rome. The armoury at Sepphoris, capital of the province of Galilee and only four miles from Nazareth, had been raided. Roman vengeance had been swift. Sepphoris burned; Jesus would have seen the flames licking the night sky. Two thousand rebels crucified; Jesus would have seen the crosses that lined the Road to the East. Men dying, their screams audible from Nazareth, the road passing beneath the cliff.

Ten-elevenths of the greatest life story in the history of mankind, the Nazareth decades, go by in silence. But they were not passed in obscurity, in a backwater. They were passed where life was raw and sometimes cruel. And life in that peasant home could not have been easy; the cheapest sacrifices for His infant Presentation tell their tale. Then the words of His manhood that reveal the memories of His boyhood. The best patch was one as old as the garment, in case the first laundering should rend it. . . .

But hard as a tekton's life was, it could not have been harder than that of an itinerant preacher. The foxes had holes and the birds of the air their nests, but the Son of Man had nowhere to call His own. In any event He thought enough of Nazareth to make a return visit.

'And he came to Nazareth, where he had been brought up; and, as his custom was, he went into the synagogue on the sabbath day, and stood up for to read.' Luke 4:16.

As His custom was. A telling phrase.

The tekton's shop of His boyhood and early manhood would have been in a street with other tradesmen's shops. You could have walked down that street on Wednesday, or Thursday, or Friday and looked into the tekton's shop, much as we did into the shop of the Arab wood carver. You would have seen Mary's sturdy firstborn deftly wielding the tools of

His trade, making His yoke or His chair, the smell of wood-shavings pleasant in the nostrils.

But visit Him on Saturday; then there would be a different story. The shop would be closed; no orders taken or delivered. It was His day of rest. You would have found Him and the remainder of His family in the synagogue, the building around which the entire town was configured. Sabbath was special.

Not surprisingly then, on His home town return, *as His custom was*, He joined the Sabbath worshippers. Of course, as time went by, things would change. But not for Jesus. At the end of the first century AD the first apostles, as they fell at their posts, warned of 'a falling away'.[1] It came. And ironically with the conversion of Roman Emperor Constantine. With Christianity the 'official religion' of the Empire, certain accommodations had to be made with heathen religious practices. Since all things Jewish were detested, the practice of worshipping on the Sun-worshippers' day was gradually adopted. Anti-Jewish sentiment had been drummed up by the Emperor Hadrian as early as AD 135. He had gone as far as to ban worship on the Sabbath, the seventh day. But the total abandonment of seventh-day worship belonged to a later century. The formal transference of the 'solemnity' from Saturday to Sunday came with the decree of the Council of Laodicea (AD 336), made by a Church so permeated with, and corrupted by heathen practices as to be unrecognizable as the outgrowth of the Church of the apostles. As always, however, a few pure spirits remained, and the seventh-day Sabbath was kept alive. Among them was the early Celtic Church. Scottish Christians worshipped on the seventh day as late as 1069.[2]

In Jesus dwelt 'all the fulness of the Godhead bodily'.[3] 'In the beginning' He was present at creation, 'and without him was not any thing made that was made.'[4] He was the Creator, and, on Sinai, the Lawgiver.[5] He spoke of 'My commandments'.[6] In the commandments He sketched man's nature by revealing him as a dependent creature, prone to evil, yet one who, by divine grace, could come to know the prohibitions as promises.

Right in the bosom of the Law was the fourth commandment which commemorated forever the towering pillars of existence, namely Creation and Redemption.[7] Here is a law that reveals the things man most needs to know – that he has an all-loving, all-powerful Heavenly Father, and that he, as the creature, needs regularly to cease from the engrossment with things that he might direct his thoughts above.

The New Testament indicates that the Sabbath is a memorial, not only of creation, but of redemption. On the sixth day Jesus cried: 'It is finished', and then rested. He could have risen the next day, but He chose to rest that Sabbath as He had rested each Sabbath of His life. Henceforth, every Sabbath would be a reminder of the finished work of redemption – a memorial of the Creator's love manifested in the re-creation of redemption.

* * *

Jesus' brief Sabbath sermon at the synagogue on His home town return visit proved controversial. A mob took Him to the scarp at the edge of which my car was now parked. But He escaped.[8]

Often during His three-and-a-half-year ministry He was involved in controversy. Again and again He risked His life and work to rescue *His* Sabbath – 'I am Lord of the Sabbath', He said[9] – from the irritating regulations of the Pharisees. Seven miracles are recorded as having taken place on the Sabbath. 'The Sabbath was made for man', He insisted.[10] Looking backward and looking forward He was saying: 'It always has been for man – and it always will be.'

* * *

With one last look at the town which, above all others on earth, felt the footprint of Jesus, we nosed the car down the precipitous slope, in second gear, right foot touching the brake.

Looking west, beyond the plain, our eyes caught the glint of the Mediterranean. That is what Sabbaths are for: far-away looks that rest, sustain and inspire the soul.

What irony that, above all the commandments, man has

forgotten the one God said to remember. And what have been the far-reaching consequences of the resultant impoverishment of body, mind and spirit . . . ?

1 2 Thessalonians 2:3. **2** Peter Geiermann, *The Convert's Catechism of Catholic Doctrine* (1957), page 50; Andrew Lang, *History of Scotland* (1900), vol. 1, page 96; Leslie Hardinge, *The Celtic Church in Britain* (1972); William Skene, *Celtic Scotland* 2nd edition (1886), vol. 2, pages 348, 349. The most comprehensive discussion of this whole question is to be found in Dr. Samuele Bacchiocchi's book, *From Sabbath to Sunday: Historical Investigation of the Rise of Sunday Observance in Early Christianity*, published in 1977 by The Pontifical Gregorian University Press. **3** Colossians 2:9. **4** John 1:1-3. **5** 1 Corinthians 10:1-4. **6** John 15:10. **7** Exodus 20:8-11. **8** Luke 4:16-30. **9** Matthew 12:8; Mark 2:28; Luke 6:5. **10** Mark 2:27.

PRESENT FOR THE FEAST

17

We were enjoying the sultry, voluptuous air of a Jerusalem late September evening. Sitting around in pools of moonlight enjoying dinner in a garden restaurant, somewhere on King David Street, we observed that the lights were unnaturally bright over the Yemin Moshe Quarter and on Mount Zion. Unlike the bright light which once dispelled the darkness of Shepherds' Fields, this was earthshine.

Later, from our vantage point high in the tower of St. Andrews, it was easy to pick out many brightly lighted areas scattered all over the city. The Jewish Quarter of the old city might have been floodlit, except that the source of the lighting was partially covered over.

Next morning, the sun not yet risen over the Mount of Olives, the earth of the Hinnom Valley still pre-dawn lavender grey, we walked by the Sultan's Pool to investigate. The glow of the previous night had gone. But, as we approached Mount Zion, we could make out strange shapes in the paling shadows.

Over the lower slopes of the mount and down in the valley to the north of the Hinnom Bridge were scores of improvised booths. Over wooden uprights were bestrewn palm and willow branches, roofs insufficient to keep out the starlight as, the night before, they had been insufficient to keep in the brightness of their artificial, unusually brilliant lights.

As we watched, men were struggling out of their booths and making for the Yemin Moshe synagogue.

What we had been observing was the commencement of a seven-day ritual which Jews from Sinai to San Francisco, from Ein Karem to Edgware had been performing for 3,500 years. It was the fifteenth day of Tishri, the seventh month of the Bible calendar. It was the Feast of Tabernacles, a feast deeply associated with both light and water. And the booths we had seen were *succoths*.

'In the fifteenth day of the seventh month,' the wandering

Israelites had been commanded, 'when ye have gathered in the fruit of the land, ye shall keep a feast unto the Lord seven days: . . . And ye shall take you on the first day the boughs of goodly trees, branches of palm trees, and the boughs of thick trees, and willows of the brook; and ye shall rejoice before the Lord . . . . all that are Israelites born shall dwell in booths.'[1]

Succoths there were in plenty on Mount Zion. Every quadrangle open to the sky contained by the sprawling building which houses King David's Tomb was taken up with *succoths*. A Jewish friend, eager that we should get the flavour of the Feast, led us from one to another and allowed us a glimpse inside; for him, however, Israel was no more than a *political* reality but, for the devout dwelling in the *succoths*, it was the realization of thousands of years of religious devotion, a close-to-messianic dream-come-true.

For these *dévots* the Feast of Tabernacles had a special significance. One of its aspects was giving thanks for the Torah, the sacred writings.

As the week progressed pitchers of water were carried, morning by morning, into the synagogues. And as blue twilight rolled like smoke down the valley, the mysterious lights shone forth from the *succoths* evening by evening.

The Feast played havoc with the traffic situation. Everywhere there were processions. And, therefore, everywhere the police were diverting motorists, but with bored disregard for intended destinations. We might be driving to the west of the city and end up, hopelessly lost, in the slums of Muslim north. By Friday driving had become a nightmare. Intent on reaching Bethany we wound our car round a police barricade. In seconds shrill whistles were sounding from all directions. Instinctively we leapt out of the car. A police sergeant, anger vein swelling, bellowed at us in Hebrew, then English. We played the idiot. With a wave of the hand which conveyed both total contempt and resignation, the sergeant allowed us to proceed.

Soon, on the Jerusalem Brigade Road which skirts the south-facing wall of the old city, we encountered the rear of a procession of Hasidim in knee-length frock coats, hats and long ringlets. By the side of the men walked miniatures of themselves, their sons in identical dress. They were making for the Western Wall by way of the Dung Gate.

We abandoned the car and watched.

From the brow of the Mount of Olives, a mile distant, we heard a great shout. Soon, winding along the ancient, narrow road down to the Kidron, opposite to the Golden Gate, we glimpsed the procession of which we had planned to be a part. They had come from Bethphage and were following the Palm Sunday route. Hymn-singing as they went, these evangelical Christians of a variety of nationalities were marching in solidarity with the Jews.

At the Western Wall thousands of Christians and Jews converged. Together they raised their voices to God in thanks for the sacred Scriptures. For both orthodox Jew and Protestant Christian the Scriptures are the divinely inspired, exclusive foundation of truth.

Thirty or so hours later found us many miles north in a hospice room in Tiberias. Shabat was over and, after having an evening walk by the Sea of Galilee, we were ready for rest. It was then that the noise began, amplified and broadcast over loud-speakers for the whole town to hear. The Feast of Tabernacles was far from our thoughts. Were we listening to the amplified sound of a midnight market, with some sort of Middle Eastern discotheque for competition? The following morning we learned that we had been the privileged auditors of the final act of The Day of the Great Hosanna, the culmination of the Feast. 'It is always an occasion for celebration and rejoicing', we were told.

* * *

In the days of Jesus, and before, Tabernacles was one of the three great feasts of the Jewish year. Tens of thousands of Jews would converge on Jerusalem, bearing with them the purple clusters of the vine and other symbols of harvest bounty. The hills and valleys around the walled city would be covered with *succoths*. At night the whole area would glow with bright light. The Temple itself would shine with what looked like supernatural illumination but would, in fact, be produced by thousands of candlesticks and flaming torches. A symbol, this, of the Sanctuary's role as a light in a world darkened by sin.

One year Jesus' brothers urged Him to attend the great feast. What was the use of being a provincial miracle worker? 'No-one who wants to become a public figure acts in secret. Since you are doing these things, show yourself to the world.' Jesus held back and His brothers and His disciples went south without Him.[2]

But in the *succoths* and the terraced streets of the capital there was one topic of conversation: the Man of Galilee. Who was He? What was He? Was it true? Where was He?

In the corridors and chambers of power the great ones plotted His murder.[3]

* * *

Each day of the Feast, at dawn, the priests had sounded a long, shrill blast upon their silver trumpets. From the *succoths* the people had answered with shouts. A specially appointed priest had been sent with a golden pitcher to draw water from the Pool of Siloam. In time with the trumpet blasts he had ascended the temple steps. Then the High Priest had poured the water, and after that a pitcher of wine, into a basin at the foot of the altar. Special conduits had conveyed the wine-mixed-with-water down to the Brook Kidron. Here, at once, was a symbol of the abundant rains the parched earth needed, cleansing from sin and an outpouring of the Holy Spirit that would follow the advent of Messiah King.[4]

* * *

The water ritual climaxed on the seventh day of the Feast, The Day of the Great Hosanna. On this day the speculation among the multitudes about Jesus had reached fever pitch.[5]

Amid the deafening blasts of a thousand trumpets and the swell of a Levite choir the water from the golden pitcher was poured. The people responded with a mighty Hallel:

'Blessed be he that cometh in the name of the Lord.'[6]

Messianic fervour engulfed the multitudes.

At the centre, a majestic figure strode forward.

It was Jesus.

He had travelled south to Jerusalem alone and in secret.[7]

The water was being poured from the golden pitcher.

His voice rang through the temple courts: *'If any man thirst, let him come unto me, and drink. He that believeth on me, as the scripture hath said, . . . shall flow rivers of living water.'*[8]

Around the walled city were the scorched hills of late summer; the blistering heat had bleached them of all colour except grim greys and sun-paled browns. An empty round of ceremonies had left the hearts of the people similarly parched for living water.

All day He taught them, until the brilliant lights shone out of the Temple at sunset.

' "I am the light of the world;" announced Jesus, "he who follows me will not walk in darkness, but will have the light of life." '[9]

* * *

Soldiers from the Temple were sent to arrest Him. They returned to their bosses without a prisoner. Furious, they said: 'Why?' The soldiers answered: 'Never man spake like this man.'[10]

The light of the world had shone into their hearts as it still shines in a sin-darkened world. And to souls parched in the wilderness of materialism the invitation is still extended: 'If any man thirst let him come unto me, and drink.' 'Let him that is athirst come. And whosoever will, let him take of the water of life freely.'[11]

1 Leviticus 23:39-43. **2** John 7:1-10, NIV. **3** John 7:11-13, 19, 20, 25, NIV. **4** E. G. White, *The Desire of Ages*, pages 448, 449; Victor Buksbazen, *The Feasts of Israel*, pages 49, 50. **5** E. G. White, op cit, pages 450-454. **6** Psalm 118:26; Victor Buksbazen, op cit, pages 50, 51. **7** John 7:10; E. G. White, op cit, page 452. **8** John 7:37, 38. **9** John 8:12, RSV. **10** John 7:44-46. **11** Revelation 22:17.

GUNFIRE FROM GOLAN

18

Up betimes we were ankle deep in Galilee, the sea blue with a *panier* of diamonds.

Five-thirty am and the fishermen were dragging their nets filled with a slippery, silver cargo onto the quay at Tiberias.

Drowsed by the already warming sun, we listened to the low chatter of shingle where the easy water was breaking.

It was on such a morning as this that Jesus recruited Simon Peter. The sun rising over the eastern hills. The snow glistening white on the peak of distant Mount Hermon. The wheezing of the ripples on the shingle. Fishermen spreading their nets to dry.[1]

What had changed in the passing of twenty centuries?

Jesus made a bee-line for Peter's boat. Climbed into it. Asked Peter to put out a little from the shore.

The hour notwithstanding, a crowd had already gathered. From His vantage point in the boat, Jesus addressed them. Some were crouching, others standing, some perched on blocks of basalt, all rapt in His words.

His speaking over, Jesus addressed Himself directly to Peter. 'Put out into deep water and let down your nets for a catch.'

Preposterous!

'Master, we were hard at work all night and caught nothing at all', came back the reply.

Peter had been brought up beside these waters. How, when and where to catch fish in Galilee; the knowledge was bred into him. This order flew in the face of all that he knew, generations of received wisdom about fishing. . . . The morning was no time for fishing – the fish could see the nets! The fish were in the shallows, not the deep! In any case, Peter must have been thinking, if I put out now the crowd will call me crazy!

If the order had not come from Jesus the reply would have been short, rude and negative.

D. LAWSON

The Church of All Nations (or the Basilica of the Agony) which encloses part of the Garden of Gethsemane.

D. LAWSON

The Citadel near the Jaffa Gate. This is the site of the palace in which Herod Antipas tried Jesus. The masonry of one of its three towers remains.

We pondered his dilemma.

Should Jesus board our ship of life He may encounter resistance. We are used to plotting our own course, being masters of our own craft. Shall we, may we, *dare we* – hand over the entire command to Him? Not knowing to where His navigation may take us, on what inhospitable terrain He may put us ashore. . . .

Peter replied: 'But if You say so, I will let down the nets.'

To rely on Christ's partnership we must sail under His orders. And those orders are often spoken in the teeth of ordinary experience and convention. To follow His orders we may have to turn our backs on the norms and conventions of the shore – and launch into deep waters.

Peter did.

Soon he was calling for assistance to get his nets to land. He clambered across from prow to stern on his bare feet, fell at the feet of Jesus and, with the heaving sobs of a strong man, confessed himself a sinner. That 'because You say so' had made the difference.

Jesus spun round on Peter: 'From now on you will be catching men.'

It would be a long time before Peter felt the pull of the water against the oars again.

* * *

The day waxed hot. The roads were white, quivering with heat.

Accompanied by a bank manager and his wife we set out to climb Mount Hermon – by car.

In the foothills, off the road to Qiryat Shemona, we discovered the excavations at Hazor. This Canaanite metropolis had been considerably larger than Jerusalem. It had been mentioned in Assyrian and Egyptian records long before the Israelite conquest in the fifteenth century BC. Joshua had been at pains to take it 'for Hazor beforetime was the head of all those kingdoms'.[2]

In the tenth century BC it had been one of Solomon's chariot towns. We examined the water system Ahab had built there and went deep down into the clammy depths of a cave to look at his water source.

Somewhere well north of Hazor our bank manager friend took over the navigation. Glancing at the map he advised sharp right up a road carved out of a mountainside. Ahead, beyond Qiryat Shemona, he reminded me, was Lebanon. There Israelis were fighting Syrians and Palestinians. We were not insured for a war zone.

Soon my sun-scalded right arm was being bathed by the cool, rarified air of higher altitudes. As the road snaked upward over the Golan Range there was a sheer drop of thousands of feet. The road was, by now, single track, and a little too narrow for comfort. The ladies in the back quailed gently, and my navigator began to speak of Wills.

There was a Druze villager by the side of the road. He was a weazened, leather-coloured old man. As he saw us, panic came into his eyes. With arm movements he indicated that we must go no further. With a swift, sharp hand movement he seemed to be indicating a precipice. We wondered if he thought we had not noticed it. Did he want us to reverse down *this* snake path?

We continued on.

Suddenly ahead there was a machine gun post and a rope across the road. An Israeli soldier brought us screeching to a halt. He was pointing a machine gun at my head. I said the first thing that leapt to mind.

'Are we anywhere near the Lebanese border?'

'Thees eez the Lebanese border', he replied. Then he smiled indulgently. Soon we were all laughing. We shared a bag of apricots and a carton of orange juice with him. Then, exercising the greatest possible care, we turned the car round and headed down mountain by the same road. Our navigator found himself on the map. In consequence he found where we had been, and where we needed to be. We were making for Banyas, the Caesarea Philippi of New Testament times. As we wound our way over the Golan Range we admired colourful Druze villages in the valleys below.

Banyas was half a square mile of rubbled heaps, almost overgrown. Scarcely a wall was standing. There was neither sight nor scent of human life. Banyas had been in comfortable range of Syrian guns in the previous Arab-Israeli war.

Above the town, in a vast wooded cleft we found that which we sought. A cavernous black hole in the mountain face, and gushing from it a mighty waterfall. This was the main source of the Jordan. This was Caesarea Philippi.

* * *

Towards the end of His ministry Jesus led twelve footsore disciples up the uneven mountain roads north from Galilee. In the course of their thirty mile up-mountain hike, feet raw and blistered, they must have wondered why. At length Galilee, below, behind them, was lost in heat mist. Ahead was the mighty mass of Hermon, and just below the summit range, Caesarea Philippi.

Perhaps it was at the waterfall where Jesus paused for a drink and confronted the disciples with His question: 'Whom do men say that I am?' After He had listened to the variety of theories as to His identity – among them Elijah, Jeremiah, John the Baptist resurrected – He put the question He had brought them thirty miles up country to ask: 'But whom say *ye* that I am?'[3]

* * *

Below the great waterfall we waded out and climbed onto a rock. We pondered His question.

Here was the main source of the Jordan. It was impossible to think of that great river and not think of the religion and history of the Jews.

Before Caesarea Philippi acquired its name it was called Baalinas, Baal's city. Even in the time of Jesus there would be ruined temples to the worship of Baal within the vicinity.

Above the town was this great cavern. The Greeks believed that their god Pan was born there. Indeed, the modern name Banyas is a corruption of the Greek name Panias.

At the time of Jesus no one could look at Caesarea Philippi without being dazzled by a temple of glistening white marble – built by the Herods to the godhead of Caesar.[4]

In a place littered with temples to Syrian gods, where Greek gods looked down, where the history of Israel crowded the mind and the landscape was dominated by the marbled-splendour of Caesar worship, a humble Galilean carpenter asked twelve very ordinary men who they believed Him to be. Against a background of the world's great religions, He demanded comparison between Him and them.

He wanted one answer, one verdict.

He got it.

From Peter.

Above the violence of that mighty waterfall it was as if his words were ringing still: *'Thou art the Christ, the Son of the living God.'*

The fishermen were called from their nets by Galilee to catch men. King David was summoned from a sheepfold to shepherd the chosen race. Paul was to be called from making goats hair tents to preach the Gospel of a house not made with hands, eternal in the heavens. Was Jesus calling us, we wondered, from our nets, benches, desks, kitchen sinks, consoles, brooms, wheels, machines – and inviting *us* to join His great adventure? If He was, then, as with Peter the customs of the shore would certainly at first cloud our thinking. . . .

Against a background of the best that the world can offer – its materialism, its ideologies, its progress, its instant experiences, its wealth, its comforts, its futility and the oblivion it offers for the hereafter – Jesus stands and invites comparison. From Caesarea Philippi through the arches of the ages, across light years and yet at our elbow He stands and asks: *'Whom do men say that I am?'*

The Theologians and Professors of Divinity leave us no shortage of answers to His question. 'The deep down in everyone's being.' 'The psychological figment necessary to fill the god-shaped blank in everyone's mind.' 'The ultimate end of man's consciousness.'

With sadness in His voice He still persists with His question: *'Whom do ye say that I am?'*

* * *

As we pulled away, not for the first time we heard the thunder of heavy artillery fire. We headed for the Golan Heights and the route down to the eastern side of Galilee.

What we found was a roadless wilderness churned up by tanks and heavy weapons of war, and baked hard by a relentless sun. Massed over miles of battleground wasteland was the hardware of Armageddon.

1 Read the story in Luke 5:1-11, NEB, and the way it is amplified by F. B. Meyer in *Peter — Fisherman, Disciple, Apostle*, pages 18-24. **2** Joshua 11:10. **3** The story of Jesus at Caesarea Philippi is to be found in Matthew 16:13-28; Mark 8:27-33; Luke 9:18-27. **4** W. Barclay, *The Daily Study Bible: Gospel of Mark*, pages 191-193.

CAPERNAUM

19

They banned me from Capernaum the first time I went there.

The day was hot beyond endurance. Only by keeping on the move in the car, air-cooler on boost, all windows down, was life supportable. I had long since shed my trousers in favour of denim shorts. And herein was the problem, said the grumpy monk who kept the gate; I was improperly dressed.

So it was that I had to content myself with wading out to sea, camera held above my head to take a few shots from the seaward side. Months later I was back. The same humourless ecclesiastic manned the gate. But the Baptist pastor who was my companion, and myself managed to done a pair of baggy trousers apiece. Our wives were, in any event, acceptably accoutred – so we sent them on ahead to buy the tickets.

What is contained within the high walls and the well guarded gate is no more than a fragment of first-century Capernaum. The town was very much larger in which Jesus called the fishermen from their nets and Matthew from his customs post, where He healed the centurian's servant and Peter's mother-in-law, where He cast a demon out of a man who challenged Him in the synagogue, brought Jairus's daughter back to life, and the town which – with Bethsaida and Chorazin – He so roundly condemned when, despite the miracles done in its environs, it failed to embrace the Gospel.[1]

There is not a trace of the first-century lakeside city of Bethsaida, home for some of the disciples. Chorazin has disappeared almost totally; there are few pre-Byzantine remains.

But Capernaum had too many solidly-built structures to disappear completely. Today ruins are being excavated over no less than a mile of coastline.

What the Franciscans have enclosed in their high wall is no more than the synagogue (partially restored) and the ruins of another large building which they claim to have been the house of Peter.

But there can be no doubt that the synagogue on its own would be worthy of a great deal of attention. Over the years, despite certain obvious indicators to the contrary, archaeologists have declined to accept that this was, in fact, the first-century synagogue in which Jesus would have preached. A variety of dates has been assigned to it well after the Resurrection.

Recently opinion has turned around dramatically. Though Capernaum's white limestone synagogue was known to have been constructed directly over an earlier one, archaeologists have dug an L-shaped trench between the stylobates. The credentials of this first-century synagogue have been established beyond reasonable doubt.[2]

Of course, there may have been more than one synagogue in first-century Capernaum. In that event we could not know in which one Jesus preached and healed. But the experts point out that the gospels always speak of 'the' synagogue. They further draw our attention to the story of Jesus healing the centurian's servant,[3] emphasizing that the correct translation of the words of those who spoke to Jesus of the centurian would be: 'He loveth our nation, and he hath built us *our* synagogue.'[4] Indeed, a careful examination of the Capernaum synagogue reveals certain decorative features in the Graeco-Roman style, doubtless incorporated by the Jewish builders in deference to the generous Roman donor.

Among the relics is a stone bas-relief. It portrays an ark – on wheels! Evidently this mobile ark was wheeled before the door of the synagogue, while the congregation faced Jerusalem in prayer.

Not far from Capernaum the red-roofed Church of the Loaves and Fishes is visible through the trees of palm and eucalyptus, the bowers of hibiscus blossoms, the walls of purple bougainvillaea and the lemon and orange trees. The stone is new, clean and white. The cool of the interior was like cold water on a parched throat. All over, masons were working on piecing together the intricate mosaic of a Byzantine floor. The new church had been built over the ruins of two Byzantine structures, the last destroyed by the Arabs in 636. The first area of the mosaic pavement was rediscovered in the present century by accident. A German priest, based at Tabgha, a keen gardener, was 'digging on the property near the lakeside and suddenly – Auchwunderbar! – he saw in the brown earth a gleam of blue and then a flash of gold and then a touch of green'.[5] Soon what had been discovered was clearly identified as loaves and fishes, indicative of the discovery of the long-lost Byzantine basilica and of the Byzantine belief that the feeding of the 5,000 took place on or near this spot.

The loaves-and-fishes mosaic is under the white stone altar of the new church. Skilled hands have now revealed other beautiful mosaics which clearly covered the entire floor area of the Byzantine basilica. We watched riveted as still more skilful hands under powerful arc lights painted Byzantine-style with Byzantine materials, the areas between the uncovered fragments – to create an incredible whole. The Byzantine grandeur restored!

Here was a work of beauty linking us with a time close to the time of Christ. And, half an hour before, we had pored over the ruins of a building in which Jesus spent many of the Sabbaths of His three-and-a-half years ministry, and had picked over the relics of a city in which He had healed the sick, cast out demons – and even restored the dead to life.

In a quiet cloister of the Loaves and Fishes basilica, my imagination racing, I was scribbling on my pad.

* * *

The disciples returned, weary but full of exploits from their two-by-two preaching ministry in the towns and villages of Galilee. Jesus called them together. 'You need a place of solitude to rest and recharge', He told them. 'Let's head out for the desert.'

But solitude was to prove elusive. A crowd saw their boat cross the lake and made its way by land to the desert retreat, a trek of at least four or five miles. The crowd numbered '5,000 men', so we may speculate as to the size of the complete multitude, including the women and children.

Inside the Carpenter-Preacher-Healer beat the heart of a Shepherd. The multitude 'were as sheep without a shepherd' and, weariness notwithstanding, Jesus could not leave His mighty flock without spiritual food and physical healing. By the time the day wore out they were on the opposite side of Galilee from the church that commemorates the miracle by which a boy's packed lunch of loaves and fishes was multiplied to feed thousands – with whole basketsful of 'fragments' left over.[6]

Souls had been stirred by the preaching of Jesus. Bodies had been healed by His touch. Now, out of a boy's packed lunch, He had fed a vast crowd of people. There was enough of the Zealot in every Galilean to know what to make of this. There arose a clamour to make Jesus king;[7] He could lead them against the garrison at Tiberias – then on to Jerusalem!

This was a delicate situation. The role Jesus had come to fill was incomparably greater than that of a freedom fighter. The sun having set over the opposite shore, the disciples were swiftly organized into their boat and told to row for Capernaum.[8] Efficiently, quietly, Jesus dispersed the multitudes. Then withdrew into the mountains to pray.

On Galilee's eastern shore, this may well have been among the mountains around Gergesa. Byzantine ruins litter a precipice there to this day. And a Byzantine basilica has been partly restored. But these commemorate the exorcism of the man among the tombs.[9]

In the night the disciples rowed against a stiffish wind.[10] Under a white moon the sea was a soft grey, shaking golden sequins among the folds of its shadows. And Jesus came walking upon the water to the astonishment of His disciples!

Not for the first time, the sea becalmed at His word.

For much of the year it is difficult to envisage Galilee as anything other than a vast millpond. But freak storms can blow down from Hermon, or howl, hurricane-like, up the fissure in the earth's crust which is the Jordan Valley. Then Galilee boils like a cauldron. Seabound from Tiberias to Ein Gev we once saw such a storm whip the mild sea into a frenzy – and prayed for a 'Peace be still' from the Master's voice.

* * *

Dawn found Jesus and His disciples at Capernaum. It also found boats from Tiberias sailing to the eastern shore of Galilee towards the stranded multitudes. Word travels fast and visibility around the inland sea is excellent. Aboard the boats from Tiberias, the crowd was soon following Jesus to Capernaum.[11]

Jesus knew that He had a serious task to accomplish. He needed to disabuse the minds of the following thousands of the misconceptions which they harboured with regard to His mission. He chose the synagogue as His venue.[12] It was packed to the doors, the cloying air heavy, moisture-full.

The point of departure for this controversial sermon was the fact that the hordes were after a rerun of yesterday's miracle-bread wonder-work. 'I am speaking of the bread that comes down from heaven, which a man may eat, and never die', He told them. 'I am that living bread . . . .'[13]

There was Messianic imagery. Was the Carpenter claiming to be God? In successive parentheses John records how the deeply spiritual words of Jesus were received by His now truculent congregation. First they 'began to murmur disapprovingly'.[14] Soon there was 'a fierce dispute' among them.[15] As He drew towards a close, even His more stalwart supporters were exclaiming, ' "This is more than we can stomach! Why listen to such talk?" '[16] 'From that time many of his disciples went back, and walked no more with him.'[17]

At first those who renounced Him would withdraw quietly, in ones and twos. Then whole groups would separate themselves from the multitude, exiting the doors of the synagogue noisily, fists upraised, fingers wagging at the Speaker. Among them would be the political hotheads, those who hoped for another free meal, then the good-hearted but narrow-minded souls who were shocked by His actual words. In no time the synagogue had emptied.

Around Jesus was the little group of aghast apostles. Yesterday they had been surfing high on the climbing wave of His popularity. Now everyone had left. They had witnessed the shattering of the Master's popularity, and they could not understand it.

There was quiet now.

Pointedly, Jesus turned to the twelve and asked: 'Will ye also go away?'

The reply came from Peter: 'Lord, to whom shall we go?'

This was no rhetorical question. There were plenty of places they could have gone. The pious people of Jesus' time went to the ritualism and legalism of the Pharisees, a convenient kind of religion. Those with a taste for solitude joined the Essenes; the Qumran monastery was one of many. The hotheads who wanted action went to the Zealots. The eggheads looked to the ideologies of the Greeks. The social climbers became hangers-on of the Sadducees, or collaborators with the Romans.

In Peter's reply was the implication that his soul craving for the bread of heaven could not be satisfied in any of these quarters.

'Lord, to whom shall we go? *thou hast the words of eternal life.*'[18]

* * *

Sitting there in a quiet cloister we thought of the empty, decaying churches back home, 'the post-Christian era'. In the quietness of that holy place we seemed again to hear the question: 'Will ye also go away?'

Shall we go to materialism, amass status symbols – fast cars, the latest gadgetry in our houses? Shall we withdraw into the fantasy world, put our minds into limbo, absorb the mental anaesthetic dished up in thirty minute helpings each evening, courtesy of the television companies? Shall we go to the higher theology – 'Jesus Christ is the eschatological manifestation of the ground of being', says the man on the TV God-slot. 'Kerygma manifested in conflict and decision in the human process'? Shall we look to politics to solve the fundamental needs of mankind – socialism, liberalism, conservatism – or any other political ism or wasm?

Lord, to whom shall we go when guilt assails us? To whom shall we go for a friend when all men forsake us? On whom shall we build our lives that the gates of hell shall not prevail against us? To whom shall we go when one by one the lights that we have trusted die out in the sky?

'Thou hast the words of eternal life.'

1 Mark 1:21-31; 2:1; 5:41; John 2:12; 4:46-54; Matthew 4:18-22; 8:14-17; 9:9-13; 11:23,

24. **2** James F. Strange and Hershel Shanks, 'Synagogue Where Jesus Preached Found at Capernaum', *Biblical Archaeology Review*, No. 9 (November/December 1983), pages 24-31. The authenticity of this synagogue as the one in which Jesus preached is accepted without reservation by, among others, Professors Robert M. Johnston and Lawrence T. Geraty of Andrews University, Berrien Springs, Michigan. **3** Luke 7:1-10. **4** Luke 7:5. **5** H. V. Morton, *In The Steps of The Master*, page 207. **6** Read the story in Mark 6:30-56; Matthew 14:13-33; Luke 9:12-17; John 6:1-21. **7** John 6:14, 15. **8** John 6:17. **9** Sylvia Mann, *The Sea of Galilee*, page 36. **10** John 6:18; Mark 6:48. **11** John 6:22-24. **12** John 6:59. **13** John 6:50, 51, NEB. **14** John 6:41, NEB. **15** John 6:52, NEB. **16** John 6:60, NEB. **17** John 6:66. **18** John 6:67, 68 (italics ours).

FUNERAL IN BETHANY

20

We had expected Bethany to be something like the Mea She-arim, but with less bustle. The mind's eye had harboured an idealized picture of a Jewish village on the quiet side of the Mount of Olives.

The Mea She-arim is an ultra-orthodox district of west Jerusalem, thick with shops, pavements thronged with grocery-laden Jews (the men do the shopping), and the narrow road blocked by groups of behatted, frock-coated, ringletted ultras in animated conversation. There are Jewish villages like this on Carmel, and at the foot of Mount Tabor.

But Bethany could not have collided more violently with our expectations. To begin with, on none of our visits have we caught sight of a single Jew, orthodox or otherwise. The village, a Sabbath-day's journey out of Jerusalem,[1] which Jesus loved to visit, has disappeared without a trace.

Perhaps quiet Ein Karem, home of Elizabeth and Zacharias, birthplace of John the Baptist, is more like the Bethany of Jesus' time. Five miles due west of Jerusalem it occupies both sides of a sheltered valley. Clean, well-cared-for churches stand on either hill: the Church of St. John and the Church of the Visitation. The latter has a huge wall with the Magnificat on marble tablets in scores of different languages. The whole village, in the season when we visited, was seemingly overgrown with flowering shrubs of every colour.

A far cry from Bethany, due east of Jerusalem, the hot breath of the wilderness scorching its narrow streets.

Shaggy, dirty sheep graze among the nettles between shanty-town dwellings. Ratty alleys separate crumbling kiosk-shops. Arab buses of unbelievable antiquity dip into their bag of gears and surge and shudder up the last incline of the road from Jericho, choking us all with dust and fumes. Occasionally small cameos of viciousness on the streets; an elderly Arab beating a donkey, a group of men in their twenties, having purposefully separated our colleague from his wife, endeavoured to molest her. . . .

We looked into one-roomed dwellings and witnessed scenes of cruel poverty. As we engaged an English-speaking septuagenarian in conversation, there was a skittering on her floor and a whole family of mice faded under the straw.

There is no shortage of 'tour guides' in Bethany. Our credulity was stretched by 'the ruins of the house of Simon the leper', 'the house of Mary, Martha and Lazarus' and 'the tomb of Lazarus'.

Over the centuries many churches have been built in Bethany. Most of them no longer exist. A single crumbling tower survives from a twelfth-century monastery. There is, however, the modern Franciscan church of St. Lazarus – surrounded by such high walls that it can only be photographed from the hill above – and a Greek orthodox monastery half a mile out of the village on the Jericho road.

One evening, returning from a search for bedouin encampments in the wilderness, the light fading, we drove towards the village. Just past the monastery we encountered a funeral, Bethany-style. The traffic was all but halted. As we drove respectfully, and at a snail's pace, past the considerable crocodile of mourners, we noticed that those at the front were carrying palm branches, and we caught sight of the embalmed corpse laid out on a board. There was no coffin.

This funeral was different, in some respects, from the one that took place in Bethany twenty centuries ago. But it had one thing, at least, in common: the gaping wound of grief, raw and bleeding.

* * *

To a man without a home, the warmth of the heart of some family where he is always welcome is precious. This was why Jesus thought so much of the home of Mary, Martha and Lazarus in Bethany. But Lazarus took sick. The sisters composed a message to Jesus: ' "Lord, the one you love is sick." '[2] Somehow they got it to Jesus, preaching, healing, miles away, outside Judea.

The message did not say, 'Come at once.' They knew that

was unnecessary. It was sufficient for Jesus to be told the fact.

When Jesus received the message He said to His disciples, ' "This sickness will not end in death. No, it is for God's glory so that God's Son may be glorified through it." '[3]

John's gospel repeatedly speaks of His glory in connection with the cross. In these words Jesus was showing His awareness that, to go to Judea, and more especially to Bethany, so close to Jerusalem, was to take a step that would end at the cross.

The disciples well knew the dangers. They remonstrated with Him. But Thomas declared his willingness to go with Him – even if it meant dying with Him.[4] Two days later Jesus and all twelve disciples started on the long road to Bethany.

' "Our friend Lazarus has fallen asleep; but I am going to wake him up" ', said Jesus. The disciples misunderstood; ' "Lord, if he sleeps, he will get better." '[5] There was no better medicine than sleep. They should have known that the word *sleep* had always had a deeper meaning for Jesus. He had said that Jairus's daughter was asleep when she was dead.[6] Perhaps they were being deliberately obtuse. Throughout the New Testament death is referred to as a sleep. At the end of Stephen's martyrdom it is said that he fell asleep.[7] Paul speaks of those who sleep in Jesus,[8] and of the witnesses of the resurrection who had subsequently fallen asleep.[9]

'So then he told them plainly, "Lazarus is dead." '[10]

When they reached Bethany Lazarus had been dead for four days. Burial followed death swiftly, and a period of seven days' mourning ensued. Jesus had arrived in the midst of this period.

Martha was out from the village to meet Him. Her heart spoke through her lips: ' "If you had been here, my brother would not have died." ' Then her faith took over: ' "But I know that even now God will give you whatever you ask." '[11]

'Jesus said to her, "Your brother will rise again." Martha answered, "I know he will rise again in the resurrection at the last day." Jesus said to her, "I am the resurrection and the life. He who believes in me will live, even though he dies; and whoever lives and believes in me will never die." '[12]

Jesus was being profound. Eternal life begins at the

moment an individual is born again. From that point on, death need have no terrors. It is no more than a sleep which ends on the great day of Resurrection. On that day – 'The Last Day' – Jesus will return in glory and wake His sleeping saints.[13]

It shocks many who examine Scripture that they can find no trace of the notion in popular theology: 'You go to heaven (or hell) when you die.' The Old and New Testaments are consistent with Jesus that death is a sleep to be broken only on the last great day of Resurrection which begins the everlasting Kingdom of God. 'The dead praise not the Lord.'[14] 'In that very day (that is, in the day of his death) his thoughts perish.'[15] 'For the living know that they shall die: but the dead know not any thing . . . their love and their hatred, and their envy, is now perished . . .'[16]

If it were any other way the resurrection of Lazarus would make no sense. Lazarus was as dead as a man could be. Jesus said so. So dead, in fact, that they buried him. They put him in a cave and rolled a great stone in front of it, after carefully preparing his body and wrapping it in the grave-clothes customary at that time.

Lazarus, one would suppose, was a good man. That being the case, according to popular theology, at the moment of his death his soul should have been freed from his body to find lodgement in heaven. On the day when Jesus resurrected him, his sister made it very clear that he had been dead for four days and that decomposition would have set in. Why call him back from the boulevards of paradise to this vale of tears? Why didn't he protest at being resurrected? Why didn't he tell Jesus that he would have preferred to remain where he was, drinking in the sights and sounds of Paradise?

Neither protest nor expressions of ecstasy broke from the lips of the resurrected Lazarus. So why the silence? A conspiracy of silence, too, perhaps? Was Jesus party to his silence about what Lazarus saw when he was light years away in heaven?

Lazarus was silent about what happened in those four days for the simple reason that nothing happened to him in those four days. His body simply began the process of returning to

Above: The Sea of Galilee south of Tiberias. The Sea of Galilee (Kinneret) lies 695 feet (212 metres) below the level of the Mediterranean. The climate is hot and humid. The sea is teeming with fish. By comparison with the time of Jesus the shoreline is relatively depopulated. On the west shore is Tiberias, and on the east the kibbutz 'Ein-Gev. Right: The Pool of Siloam, one end of the 1,750-foot (533-metre) tunnel hacked out of living rock during the reign of Hezekiah, 728-699 BC.

A. R. RODD

Above: The Garden Tomb. Outside is a groove in which a great stone was once rolled into position. Right: A walkway – built around 150 BC – which constituted one of the main streets of Jerusalem at the time of Jesus.

the dust from which mankind is created. When he was restored to life, that process was halted and reversed and Christ gave him the breath of life again. And he became 'a living soul' (as the Bible puts it in Genesis 2:7).

* * *

Another figment of popular theology is the concept of an ever-burning hell. The Bible knows nothing of 'the hot place' as it is caricatured. True enough that, in foretelling the coming judgement to follow His return in glory, Jesus said: 'Then shall he say also unto them on his left hand, Depart from me, ye cursed, into everlasting fire.'[17] But reference to the Greek text leads us in the opposite direction from the concept of an everlasting holocaust. Instead there is the idea that the *results* of the fires of judgement are permanent, everlasting. Eternal death is not a painful form of eternal life.

* * *

With Martha and Mary, and the company of mourners from the home, Jesus and His disciples went to the tomb on the wilderness outskirts of the village. The Greek text indicates that 'such deep emotion seized Jesus that an involuntary groan was wrung from His heart.'[18] He wept. The crowd was astounded at His anguish.[19] Jesus suffers as we suffer. His grief is in our grief.

Then the voice of Jesus rang out echoing endlessly across that empty wilderness, shuddering the power of death and making the very devil tremble: *'Lazarus, come forth.'* 'And he that was dead came forth, bound hand and foot with grave-clothes.'[20]

* * *

Even in our 'post-Christian era' when death strikes we are pulled up with a jolt. We are conscious that there is a void in our lives; that there are questions in our minds for which we have never received convincing answers. And we ask ourselves, Is death 'the final curtain'? If so, what is the meaning of life?

Part of our nature simply refuses to accept that life is no

more than 'a bagatelle of transient experience'. If death is indeed 'the final curtain', the end of everything, then life is devalued, and man no more than self-deluded, animated dust.

The Christian knows that, though death may run the most robust of us down, it need hold no terrors for him. Man is born, lives, grows and may pass away, but he has roots among eternal things. Through and over the stampede of the passing years God is God from everlasting to everlasting. His promises stand firm though all things perish.

'We wish you not to remain in ignorance . . .', says Paul, 'about those who sleep in death.' And with good reason; for on this all-important question turns also the significance of *life*. He continues: 'You should not grieve like the rest of men, who have no hope. We believe that Jesus died and rose again; and so it will be for those who died as Christians . . . .'[21]

On the strong and sufficient evidence of an empty tomb in an Easter garden, and of a risen Lord walking and talking and eating with men along evening roads of sadness to wide boulevards of joy, is based the Gospel of an ever-open future. That, though a man dies, believing in Jesus he has a title to eternity and will rise again – because Jesus rose again.

'I am the Resurrection and the Life . . .' Jesus still says. He is the Source and Home of life. Above the stampede of the passing years faith breathes 'Thou remainest. Thy years fail not. From everlasting to everlasting Thou art God. And death itself dies beneath Thy touch.'

* * *

They called a special meeting of the Sanhedrin to consider the resurrection of Lazarus. A miracle worker with the power to destroy death might also destroy the entire Jewish establishment. Should the Romans become aware of such a man *they* might move in and sweep that establishment away. The high priest, Caiaphas, stood up and put the matter bluntly. Better, he argued, that one Man should die than the whole nation perish. This is the argument commonly used to justify the execution of martyrs, but in this case Caiaphas spoke truer words than he knew, for Jesus' death was to save, not just a nation, but mankind.[22]

1 One and five-eighths of a mile or 15 stadia. **2** John 11:3, NIV. **3** John 11:4, NIV. **4** John 11:16. **5** John 11:11, 12, NIV. **6** Matthew 9:24. **7** Acts 7:60. **8** 1 Thessalonians 4:13. **9** 1 Corinthians 15:6. **10** John 11:14, NIV. **11** John 11:21, 22, NIV. **12** John 11:23-25, NIV. **13** 1 Thessalonians 4:13-18. **14** Psalm 115:17. **15** Psalm 146:4. **16** Ecclesiastes 9:5, 6. **17** Matthew 25:41. **18** William Barclay, *Commentary on the Gospel of John*, vol. 2, page 97. **19** John 11:35, 36. **20** John 11:43, 44. **21** 1 Thessalonians 4:13, 14, NEB. **22** John 11:45-50, NIV.

NOT ONE STONE!

21

If blood were indelible old Jerusalem would be red, all red. And in no part would it have soaked deeper than on Temple Mount.

First called Mount Moriah this mount overlooked the confluence of the Kidron and Hinnom valleys. In the valley extending south from the present-day city, the most ancient settlement was situated. And, to Moriah above it, then a rocky outcrop, God called Abraham from Hebron to learn the meaning of redemption.[1]

With the Israelite invasion under Joshua, Jericho had fallen, but not Jerusalem. Lands to both north and south of the city were appropriated to the tribes at Shiloh,[2] but the Hebrews had no capital. It remained for David years later, the second and greatest of their kings, to take it from the Jebusites.[3] Having taken it he built his own city, now the subject of fascinating excavations.

Still it was towered over by craggy Mount Moriah. Here, where Abraham had learned of a Redeemer to come from God typified by a lamb,[4] David built an altar for the sacrifice of lambs.[5]

The golden age for both the city and the mount was under David's heir, Solomon. The city was extended. On Mount Moriah, where the Dome of the Rock – erected in AD 688 after Jerusalem's surrender to Muslim Khalif Omar – now covers the site of the altars of Abraham and David, Solomon built a Temple. Where the silver-domed El Aksa mosque now stands, he built a palace. Near present-day Damascus Gate there is a vast underground cavern from where stone for the Temple was quarried.[6] The temple was panelled with cedar from Lebanon and floored with gold. In the palace was an ivory throne overlaid with gold and, in the stables below, stalls for 4,000 horses.[7] But the armies of Nebuchadnezzar destroyed all.

When Nehemiah returned from exile in Persia with his

band of masons, Jerusalem was rubbled. In the years that followed, the walls, the Temple, and the city were rebuilt. More bloodshed and slaughter came with the Romans, who left Herod the Great, an Idumaean not a Jew, as their vassal king. Irony of ironies, it was he who built the magnificent Temple – on Mount Moriah again – of the time of Jesus.

The 'platform' on which the Temple was built was extended to twice its previous size. Vast retaining walls were constructed around this platform. The lower layers of what is known as the Western Wall formed part of this retaining wall that fronted on the Tyropoeon Valley, now largely filled in. The main structure of the south-east corner of the old city walls is also from Herodian masonry, a part of Herod's retaining wall on the Kidron side of the Temple. Within the enlarged area of 351 yards north side, 512 yards east side, 536 yards west side and 309 yards south side was erected one of the finest buildings in the ancient world.

On many occasions we have stood on the great paved area surrounding the two magnificent Muslim mosques and tried to recapture in our imaginations that once great Temple of the Jews. But the imagination is stirred instead by the splendid gold and silver crescent-topped domes, the incredibly beautiful mosaics which overlay the outer walls of the Dome of the Rock – and the tremendous sweep of Mount Scopus and the Mount of Olives of which Temple Mount affords a heartlifting vista.

To recapture for the imagination Herod's great Temple, and the city of which it was part, a long trek is necessary. Across West Jerusalem, past the vast apartment buildings of wealthy Ashkanazim, to the south-western edge of the modern city. Here the great road winds towards a coast between olive groves. On one of the undulations in the gradual decline from the mountain capital, is situated the Holyland Hotel. In its grounds is a vast model of Jerusalem in AD 66. It was built after a careful examination of historical sources by reputable scholars and in materials used at the time. We picked out the Antonia Fortress, Herod's great palace, the pools of Siloam and Bethesda, grander by far in those days, great villas and centres of entertainment for the Romans – and the last

Temple of the Jews. Corinthian columns in bronze, a variety of courts and gates, gleaming, spacious cloisters, the snow-white marble of the terraced courts . . .

. . . Our imaginations thus fired, the centuries dissolve and we are following Jesus and His disciples as they exit the Golden Gate towards the Kidron Valley, heads turned back to the glories behind them . . . . The gigantic foundation stones, some sixty feet long, gates faced with gold, silver and brass . . .

' "Your house",' Jesus had proclaimed to the Jewish establishment, ' "is left to you desolate." '[8]

Remembering these words, then admiring the vast edifice, the pride of the nation, one disciple said: ' "Look . . . What massive stones! What magnificent buildings." '[9]

All *this* left desolate . . . ?

' "Not one stone here will be left on another; every one will be thrown down" ', insisted Jesus.[10]

The disciples now looked uncomfortable, eyes darted hither and yon for Temple spies. This was treason talk. Best get Jesus away.

On a terrace of olive and fig trees on the other side of the Kidron they rested. Not for the first time they watched the sunset behind the pinnacles, stairways and gilded gates of the Temple. The sky was alive, running with immense streams of flame. Then as the sun went down it seemed to drag the whole sky with it like the shreds of a burning curtain. . . .

Assured of privacy, a disciple enquired urgently: 'Tell us, when shall these things be? and what shall be the sign of thy coming, and of the end of the world?'[11]

Jesus *could* have corrected their misconception immediately. It was natural for them to think that the destruction of Jerusalem could only take place at the end of the world. But it was not to be. The two events would be separated by many centuries. But Jesus did not disabuse them.

He answered the question conscientiously.

There would be specific signs which would indicate that the fall of Jerusalem was imminent.

There would be signs which would have a *primary* application in their own lifetime, preceding Jerusalem's fall, and a *secondary* application in a much later age, preceding the return of Jesus in glory and the establishment of His everlasting Kingdom.

The disciples could expect the City's imminent fall when they saw, ' "standing in the holy place 'the abomination that causes desolation', spoken of through the prophet Daniel." '[12] The 'abomination' in the mind of Jesus, as that prefigured by Daniel, was the legions of Rome. When the legions appeared the only recourse was flight to the mountains on the other side of the Jordan. And they should pray that their flight would not be in the winter, when the weather would be foul and the Jordan in flood, nor on the Sabbath, when their worship would be disturbed.[13] This latter allusion is interesting; Jesus expected that many years into the Christian era His followers would still be observing the Sabbath of the fourth commandment.

But the appearance of the legions was the signal for flight.

Before they appeared there would be other signs, signs which would find a secondary application far down the centuries. For His followers, Jesus intended them as both indicators and warnings.

There would be 'false Christs'.[14] Forewarned, no Christian was involved in risings in favour of Theudas or an Egyptian charlatan which took place between the Resurrection and the Fall of Jerusalem.

There would be 'wars and rumours of wars', but they were not to be troubled.[15] The Pax Romana which obtained under Caesar Augustus at the birth of Christ ended after the Resurrection. The historian Tacitus says that the period was 'stained with the blood of battles, embroiled with dissensions, and horrible even in the intervals of peace'.

Jesus went on to speak of an increased incidence of natural disasters like famines and earthquakes. He warned them that they would be persecuted because they were followers of His. That some would suffer martyrdom.[16] The historical record bears out the warning: there was a devastating famine in Judea during the reign of Claudius Caesar, earthquakes and epidemics in the Aegean region, Macedonia, Asia Minor and even in Rome itself. The infant Church was hounded and persecuted. Some, like Stephen, suffered death. Paul was hauled before Gallio, Felix, Festus and Agrippa – and was finally beheaded by the orders of Nero in Rome. 'Vast multitudes', according to Tacitus, were butchered in a general persecution associated with the name of Nero.

'The days of vengeance', foretold by Jesus, were brought about when the Zealots, after driving the Roman garrison from Jerusalem, organized a national uprising. In AD 66 Nero sent a great army under Vespasian to visit vengeance upon the Jews. Vespasian, fresh from triumphs in Britain, began his campaign in the north.

As the Roman army slaughtered its way south, Vespasian heard news from Rome. He left it in the command of his 28-year-old son Titus – and left for Rome himself. He was soon to be declared Emperor.

Hence it was Titus who, in AD 70, appeared with the fifth, tenth, twelfth and fifteenth Roman legions around Jerusalem.

But the Christians were spared the horrors of the siege and the butchery of the capitulation. Mindful of the words of Jesus they fled for the mountains. Behind them was a doomed city; they made their way to Pella, south of the Sea of Galilee, a place now called Kherbet-el-Fahil. Their flight occurred before the onset of winter and there is reason to believe that it was on some other day than the Sabbath. Not one Christian life was lost in the Fall of Jerusalem in which, if Josephus Flavius is to be believed, hundreds of thousands of Jews perished. Ninety thousand more were sent into slavery. Others escaped to join the Diaspora, and in the succeeding centuries Jewish communities were to be found in many countries of the world.

When the city was taken at first it was the intention of Titus to preserve 'this marvellous magnificence', the Temple. Nevertheless, in the course of the fighting, flaming braziers were thrust against the cedar doors of the Temple area. In the vast conflagration that ensued the gold and silver coverings melted, the Holiest of Holy places was desecrated by Roman soldiers and a burning brand left behind to destroy it. At length the walls fell in, cedar-wood roofing collapsing in a vast inferno – and not one stone was left upon another.

Zealots fought on and only when total slaughter was in prospect did a small group succeed in escaping to Masada, Herod's mountain citadel by the Dead Sea.

1 Genesis 22:1-18. **2** Joshua 18:1, et seq. **3** 2 Samuel 5:6-10. **4** Genesis 22:8, 13. **5** 1 Chronicles 21:2, 17; 2 Samuel 24:18, 25. **6** Charles Gulston, *Jerusalem*, page 61. **7** ibid. **8** Matthew 23:38, NIV. **9** Mark 13:1, NIV. **10** Matthew 24:2, NIV. **11** Matthew 24:3. **12** Matthew 24:15, NIV. **13** Matthew 24:20. **14** Matthew 24:5. **15** Matthew 24:6. **16** Matthew 24:7-11.

A GREAT EXPECTATION

22

Facing the sunset-framed Temple Jesus pursued His Olivet Sermon.

The Temple would be destroyed; not one stone left upon another. That had come as a bombshell to the little coterie of disciples seated, heads bent forward, under the fig trees. Deeply disturbed, one of them pressed Jesus for more information; *'What shall be the sign of thy coming, and of the end of the world?'* [1]

His reply was of vital concern because it is recorded in great detail by Matthew, Mark and Luke.[2] But in all three accounts there is an interweaving of two strands. The context of the disciple's question indicates that, in his mind, the Fall of Jerusalem and the coming of Jesus 'at the end of the world' were one and the same thing. In the detailed account of indicators and warnings given by Jesus by way of reply, the interweaving of signs of a city's destruction and of the world's destruction is such as to make a separation of the two strands very difficult. Unless, that is, the simple principle explained in the last chapter is accepted: that many of the signs would have a *primary* application before the Fall of Jerusalem; and a *secondary*, and far wider application during 'the time of the end' before the coming of Christ in glory.

To assume that not only the questioner, but Matthew, Mark, Luke – and Jesus were confused, if not mistaken, regarding the Fall of Jerusalem and the Return is not an option.

The whole of Scripture rustles with the rumour of apocalypse. The concepts of the Olivet Sermon reflected the prophecies of Daniel, Joel and Isaiah, among others.

As certain verses in the sermon referred entirely and specifically to the Fall of Jerusalem, certain other verses referred equally entirely and specifically to the Second Advent.

In Matthew's account, in his 24th chapter, verses 14 and 27 are good examples.

In verse 14 (NIV) Jesus foretells that ' "this gospel of the kingdom will be preached in the whole world as a testimony to all nations" ' before 'the end'.

Verse 27 (NIV) could not possibly be confused with the Fall of Jerusalem. ' "For as the lightning comes from the east and flashes to the west, so will be the coming of the Son of Man." '

One New Testament verse in every twenty-five refers directly to the Second Advent, the most graphic accounts being found in the writings of Paul (in particular to the Thessalonians), Peter (his second epistle) and John (in the book of Revelation).

In John's gospel we find Jesus, speaking to the disciples in the upper room on the night of His betrayal, giving the specific assurance, 'I will return.'[3]

Standing on trial before high priest Caiaphas, and under oath, Jesus said: 'I say unto you, Hereafter shall ye see the Son of man sitting on the right hand of power, and coming in the clouds of heaven.'[4]

In the account of the ascension, while the disciples still looked wonderingly after their Lord and Saviour as He receded from view, 'two men dressed in white stood beside them.' They said: ' "Men of Galilee . . . why do you stand here looking into the sky? This same Jesus, who has been taken from you into heaven, will come back in the same way you have seen him go into heaven." '[5]

Putting together all the New Testament references to the Second Coming it is possible to obtain an over-all picture. Jesus said that the timing of His Coming was God's secret, and that speculation was useless.[6] He could not have made it clearer that the Coming would be no hole-in-the-corner affair, but that it would be a cosmic spectacle beyond the vocabulary of man to describe. Everyone would see it.[7] Paul makes it equally clear that the Coming would also be accompanied by a grand resurrection; 'One word of command, one shout from the archangel, one blast from the trumpet of God and the Lord himself will come down from Heaven! Those who have died in Christ will be the first to rise, and then we who are still living will be swept up with them into the clouds to meet the

Lord in the air. And after that we shall be with him for ever.'[8]

* * *

There can be no doubt that the great expectation left to His followers by Jesus under the evening sky only days before His crucifixion kindled their courage and inspired their vision in the age of persecution which shortly broke upon them.

Three buildings around the summit of the Mount of Olives remind us of the Blessed Hope handed down to future generations of Christians to our own day.

When you have swapped jests with the schoolboy postcard sellers, the vendors of assorted olive wood bric-a-brac and the Ali Baba look-alikes with their self-hire camels, then it is possible to enter the Dome of the Ascension. Originally built in AD 380 it is an octagonal structure, at the centre of which is a rock which bears a footprint.

Nearby is the Tower of the Ascension. This building dominates the skyline of the Mount of Olives and of Jerusalem itself. From the east it can be seen for miles across the Wilderness of Judea. Were it possible to climb it, it would afford the finest views in Israel. Despite attempts to reach it made over many weeks, and the efforts of assorted guides and advisers to enable us to enter, we eventually had to give up on our ambition to visit this great landmark. It is situated within the high walls of a Russian compound. The Russian sisters who inhabit the convent within the grounds do not welcome visitors.

But one nearby church was erected specifically to commemorate the Olivet Sermon. Beneath it, under a shelf of rock, is a cavernous grotto where Jesus is traditionally believed to have preached the sermon in which He promised to return. It represents the earliest Christian shrine on the Mount of Olives, and was erected in AD 333. Today the Carmelite church which covers the grotto is called the Church of the Pater Noster. In its peaceful, arched cloisters will be found marbled on the walls the Lord's prayer in forty-four different languages.

* * *

The disciple's words still haunt us; *the sign of Thy Coming and of the end of the world*. We remember the first application of the signs described by Jesus. Their fulfilment up to the Fall of Jerusalem confirms our faith in His prophecy. But He had more, much more, in mind than the destruction of Jerusalem. He was outlining for the benefit of generations of believers yet unborn, more especially for end-time believers, the signs that would indicate that His return in glory was imminent.

We examined the primary application of these signs in the last chapter.

Let us see if they have a wider, secondary application – perhaps for our own day.

* * *

Many of the indicators Jesus mentioned – wars, famines, earthquakes – have been endemic since His own time. But then He did not say, 'Every time there is a war tell all and sundry that I am about to return.' What He *did* say was: 'Don't be alarmed. Such things must indeed happen, but that is not the end . . . all that is only the beginning of the birth-pangs' of the new age.[9]

But it pulls us up with a jolt when we begin to realize that, in *our* century, history has shifted its gears. The vehicle is travelling at a lunatic pace. The incidence of signs mentioned by Jesus has increased by geometric proportions. The sheer *scale* of the problems Jesus predicted is such that sober-sided scientists say: This must have an end. And the great thinkers of our day: The most depressing thought possible is this disease-racked, starving, nuclear-menaced, violence-pummelled, polluted planet in unending existence.

1. *Jesus warned against deceivers in the area of religion, 'false Christs', 'false prophets'.*[10] And we live in an age of charlatans. Forewarned is forearmed! said Jesus. There has been a whole army of gurus, necromancers and purveyors of ESP and the occult, mediums, many of whom 'show signs and wonders'. There are those who claim Christian credentials, but fail to preach the simple Gospel. There are those who advocate Christian teaching mixed with practices which have their roots in heathenism. These, too, are charlatans. 'You

have been warned! Beware!' says Jesus.

2. *Jesus warned of wars.*[11] The wars the disciples lived to see were skirmishes by comparison with the two world wars of the present century. And they, in turn, have been entirely left behind by the vast potential of the superpower nuclear stockpiles. To a generation over which global annihilation looms large Jesus says: ' "Men's courage will fail completely as they realize what is threatening the world, for the very powers of heaven will be shaken. Then men will see the Son of Man coming in the cloud with great power and splendour! But when these things begin to happen, stand up, hold your heads high, for you will soon be free." '[12]

3. *Jesus warned of famines and epidemics.*[13] Between thirteen and twenty million children die annually from malnutrition. In a world where every year there are eighty million more mouths to feed, the spectre of starvation haunts the entire planet. Societies weakened by starvation are easy targets for epidemics. Medical science has made its conquests; but the most stubborn diseases resist its efforts, and the sheer scale of epidemics in the Third World are beyond its capability to treat.

4. *Expect earthquakes, said Jesus.*[14] And there have *always* been earthquakes. But in the twentieth century there have been more major earthquakes recorded than in the previous 1,900 years combined. And it's not just a case of more sophisticated recording equipment; historians and scientists have kept a careful tally of major upheavals in the earth's crust, yet it is only in the past few decades that the frequency has shown a major, in fact a staggering upturn.

5. *'As lawlessness spreads, men's love for one another will grow cold',*[15] *said Jesus.* Had He foreseen the breakdown of the family, the rejection of all standards of morality, the threat to law and order, the uninhibited vandalism, the sheer selfishness, lust and greed of our own generation?

6. *Dramatic celestial phenomena will appear before My return, said Jesus.*[16] And He provided details of what these celestial phenomena would be. The Dark Day of 19 May 1780 and the falling of the stars on 13 November 1833, and other unusually large meteorite showers since that date, have

been seen by some as complete, by others as partial, fulfilments of this prophecy.

7. *My Gospel will reach every nation on earth before the epic day dawns, said Jesus.*[17] The message of salvation by grace through faith in Jesus Christ alone and of the coming Kingdom of God will be presented on a world scale, before the Return.

* * *

Days away was crucifixion, resurrection, ascension and the birth and rapid growth of the Christian Church. Forty years away was the Fall of Jerusalem. But in this apocalyptic sermon in an Olivet evening Jesus was peering down the centuries to a dark end-time age. He was hearing the sounds as of a million trumpet blasts shattering the routines and obsessions of earth. He was seeing a huge shaft of dazzling light funnelling through the weeping blackness of what man had made of the world – swelling, expanding, dilating: and in the midst His return to earth as King of kings to put an end to suffering, starvation, sorrow and death, and to usher in His eternal Kingdom.

Perhaps He glanced one last time at the glimmering lights of old Jerusalem over the Kidron Valley. Perhaps He saw the successive destructions of that city over twenty centuries. Perhaps He saw, as did John the Revelator, 'the holy city, new Jerusalem, coming down from God out of heaven, prepared as a bride adorned for her husband'[18] – the habitation of the faithful.

1 Matthew 24:3. **2** Matthew 24; Mark 13; Luke 21. **3** John 14:1-3. **4** Matthew 26:64. **5** Acts 1:9-11, NIV. **6** Matthew 24:36. **7** Matthew 24:26, 27, 30, 31; Revelation 1:7. **8** 1 Thessalonians 4:15-18, Phillips. **9** Matthew 24:6-9, Phillips. **10** Matthew 24:4, 5, 11, 23-27. **11** Matthew 24:6, 7. **12** Luke 21:25-28, Phillips. **13** Matthew 24:7. **14** Matthew 24:7. **15** Matthew 24:12, NEB. **16** Matthew 24:29. **17** Matthew 24:14. **18** Revelation 21:2.

HOLOCAUST

23

They call it Yad Vashem.

The name is taken from the words of an ancient seer; 'Even unto them will I give in mine house . . . a place and a name . . . .' Isaiah 56:5.

'Even unto them . . . .'

To whom?

To six million European Jews who perished in the Nazi Holocaust. For this is the Hall of Remembrance built on the Mount of Remembrance, away from the grim, alluring seethe of West Jerusalem. Here the Eternal Flame burns in its broken, bronze cup *lest we forget*.

Outside, an offensively vast platform of concrete seems to be crushing the walls of small, grey basalt boulders, symbols of the Mountains of Skulls. And there is the sculpture, unnervingly real; electric fences, wire cruelly barbed, and parchment skin, stretched over bone-frames recognizably human, hanging upon it.

In the eerie, bluish half-light of the breathless interior Hasidim in knee-length frock coats silently rub shoulders with the bejeaned and bejewelled Jews of the Diaspora, eyes swimming – and Western goyim like us.

Out of the liquid blue-grey light, among tall, shuffling shadows, is the deathly pallor of the images the world must never be allowed to forget . . .

. . . the blood-covered corpses of Buchenwald, fear frozen in unseeing eyes . . . the horizontally tiered bunks, layer on layer, no more than eighteen inches apart, and those skeletal faces, bulging staring eyes ennerved with terror, waiting . . .

. . . Dachau and more huddled masses of humanity dehumanized . . . the extermination building, the first room full of sickeningly skinny naked bodies under a shower . . . then another apparent shower room with waterless showerheads in the ceiling but no drains: a gas chamber . . . a stack of corpses with a guard pulling re-usable gold and silver from the mouths

Right: The Good Friday procession along the Via Dolorosa and (left) the Latin Calvary in the Church of the Holy Sepulchre.

Dawn over Galilee, sky and sea silver with mounting sun.

of the dead . . . then the ovens, rusted slides pulled out as if waiting for more bodies . . . and the entrance to Dachau, the words *Never Again* in five languages . . .

. . . Babi Yar, a great chasm near Kiev; and in the chasm three hundred thousand bodies massacred by the Nazis, many of them in a single day . . . shot, group by shuffling group . . . methodically dumped into that chasm . . . .

* * *

Now the chasm is closed, the bodies buried, the soil smoothed.

Dachau is a museum to an age truncated in time when the world went mad, and the words *Never Again* are all the assurance we seem to need that the madness will never recur. In our warm, well fed, comfortable world we ignore the evidence that the madness is ongoing, that the words over Dachau's entrance are idle and that the chasm is yawning wide open . . .

. . . out of many a Third World chasm they stumble on reed-thin legs, exhausted mothers cradling hollow-eyed children with death's-head faces, their limbs as thin and fragile as dried twigs . . .

. . . under many a totalitarian regime they are tortured, imprisoned without trial, committed to psychiatric institutions for 'corrective therapy' if they hold the 'wrong opinions' – or disappear without a trace . . .

. . . on our very doorstep in this privileged land the chasm yawns – and more and more of the dead and maimed fall into is as the months go by . . .

. . . there are the one hundred and one political hot spots where wars, civil wars, forgotten wars rage on, pushing hundreds of thousands – the physically and mentally maimed, the dead, civilian, military – into a bottomless chasm . . . more bodies for the chasm and no soil is smoothed over *this* chasm, and no Yad Vashems are built for *these* victims; but they too have a name – and a place in the heart of God . . .

. . . while, in underground silos, the superpowers prepare to blast open the biggest chasm of all. . . .

* * *

Is there an alternative to the chasm? Can we avoid the *final* holocaust?

* * *

Let us join Jesus and eleven of His disciples in an upper chamber: the eve of 14 Nisan, AD 31.

In Old Jerusalem they called it the Upper City. We call it Mount Zion.

From the upper chamber they looked across city roofs to the dark shape of the Antonia Fortress. Pilate and Claudia were in residence for the great Jewish Feast.

Herod Antipas, down from Galilee, had caused a stir when he had arrived at the palace on the west-facing wall.

Down the old Maccabean street, beyond the Brook Kidron, was the olive garden. The dark outline of the trees was just visible on the foothills of the Mount of Olives. No moonbeams penetrated there.

Around the city, the hills were dotted with the camp fires of the pilgrims. Except to the north. North of the city was Mount Moriah's northernmost outcrop. Here, where the great road struck north there were no camp fires. These hills had traditionally been reserved for pilgrims from Samaria. And they had long since ceased to attend the Feast of the Passover. Thus they had left the only empty space around the crowded hills and valleys beyond the walls where an execution could take place. This fact was to give a sinister significance not many hours hence to a hill not many yards from the great road.[1]

But in the upper chamber on Mount Zion, eleven men were breathless. A feeling of gloom weighed on them. It was as if time was ebbing towards its close.

Hours away was the arrest in the olive garden where no moonbeams shone.

The high priest's house, down mountain, would be the scene of a sham trial in the small hours.

In Herod's palace, the Man who now reclined with His disciples on couches around a U-shaped table would be ridiculed.

He would stand before the Roman governor in Antonia first light of the following morning.

For now, though, there was only the apprehension of gloom, and physical fear. Hearts turned to ice and bowels to water.

Jesus was saying: 'Let not your hearts be troubled: . . . I will come again, and take you to Myself, that where I am you may be also. And you know the way where I am going.'

In the intimate atmosphere of that little, final gathering Thomas found the courage to say, 'Lord, we do not know where You are going; how can we know the way?'

In reply he heard Jesus say, 'I am the Way.'[2]

It was, therefore, the most natural thing that His followers should become known as 'the followers of the Way'.

When He had left behind, empty, the new tomb in a garden near the place where He was crucified,[3] and, within a few hundred yards of this accessible, incontrovertible fact His followers had begun to preach the pardon, peace and joy which came through His death and resurrection, they were preaching the Way.

Their preaching met with outstanding results. Palestine was shaken by the new Way, and the news reached Syria. One fire-eater asked the authorities 'for letters to the synagogues at Damascus, so that if he found any belonging to the Way, men or women, he might bring them bound to Jerusalem.'[4]

But, before he reached Damascus, Saul the persecutor had an encounter on the road with Jesus the Way, and, renamed Paul, became the most active champion of the Way in the first century. As a result of his irrepressible activities in Asia, it was said that 'there arose no little stir concerning the Way'.[5] The nuisance value of Paul to the Roman Empire was such that he was imprisoned and tried before Tertullus, He was tried, too, before Felix, described as 'having a rather accurate knowledge of the Way'.[6] At the end of the day it is likely that Paul was forced to defend his belief in the Way before Nero himself, a lonely experience, but, said Paul, 'The Lord stood by me.'

* * *

Back to the upper chamber on Mount Zion.

Here, with the Passover moon rising, and with the apprehension of storms soon to break, the disciples listened to the final urgent encouragement of Jesus about the Way.

'Anyone who has faith in me will do what I have been doing. He will do even greater things than these . . .'[7]

He had never taught outside Palestine. His followers would preach the triumphs of the cross to the perimeters of the known world.

'If you love Me, you will keep My commandments.'[8]

The love demanded by Jesus of the followers of the Way was not sentiment. He was about to die an excruciating death on Skull Hill – that the sin and self-life of the followers of the Way might die with Him. Love so amazing, so divine would demand life, soul, all, in obedience.

In the breathless Nisan evening in that upper room, a lamp hanging on the ceiling casting a flickering light, He promised the followers of the Way a more profound peace than the world could understand – and a joy that no one could take away from them.[9]

Then He let slip the greatest secret of all. A victorious champion of the Way must spend each day in the company of Him who is the Way, 'abide in Him' as a branch draws sap from the vine.[10] Strength and power would come from daily communion, from ingesting His Word, and from the indwelling of His Spirit.[11] Before praying one last prayer and then leading them on down the terraced Maccabean street to the olive garden where no moonbeam shone, there was one last word, hurriedly uttered, that none would ever forget: 'In the world you have tribulation; be of good cheer, I have overcome the world.'[12]

Those first followers of the Way were to see that the world could do its worst to the Way and not defeat Him. 'My victory can be your victory', He was saying. 'The world will do its worst to Me and I will emerge victorious. So can you, whatever they do to you. The courage and conquest of the Way is all yours.'

* * *

On the bottom line there is a choice of two directions in life.

The first says, 'Life is a dusty scuffle over a parched terrain – meaningless. The human race is a planetary eczema, each member no more than an enlarged protein molecule. Life, matter and time, which began by chance, will end by chance – whether by bang or whimper.' That is the philosophy of the Chasm. Set against this is the alternative to the Chasm, the philosophy of the Way; 'For God so loved the world that he gave his only Son, that whoever believes in him should not perish, but have eternal life.'[13]

* * *

At the end of the day, then, a choice.
A choice –
between purpose and futility,
aim and aimlessness,
love and self.
A choice – between the Chasm and the Way.

1 S. W. McBirnie, *The Search for the Authentic Tomb of Jesus* (1975), pages 71-72, 140-141. **2** John 14:1-8. **3** John 19:41. **4** Acts 9:2, RSV. **5** Acts 19:23, RSV. **6** Acts 24:22, RSV. **7** John 14:12, NIV. **8** John 14:15, RSV. **9** John 14:27; 16:22. **10** John 15:4. **11** John 14:16, 17, 26. **12** John 16:33, RSV. **13** John 3:16, RSV.

LEST I FORGET GETHSEMANE

24

What can we say about Gethsemane?

On two sides there are roads; the main Jericho road *around* the Mount of Olives and the ancient, narrow road *over* the Mount which once bore Jesus in triumph to Jerusalem. A stiff walk up from the Brook Kidron, it is still on the lower slopes of the Mount. Walled in on three sides, the Basilica of the Agony – the Church of the Nations – flanks it on the fourth. The basilica encloses a large part of the original garden, including a cragged area of bare rock.

The only entrance is from the narrow Palm Sunday road. We have never been able to reach it without running the gauntlet of half a hundred high-pressure trinket salesmen. But inside, walls overgrown with bougainvillaea and honeysuckle, their din is inaudible.

There is peace, reverence, serenity – and timelessness. A carpet of tiny flowers in every colour covers the area beneath eight gnarled olive trees of fantastic age. Looking at them it was natural to share the hope of our Franciscan guide that they were the very trees that witnessed the agony. It is a fact that no olive tree dies without sending forth shoots for a new tree. Perhaps these were the children of the originals. Beyond them, atop the opposite wall of the Kidron Valley, is the bricked-up Golden Gate. By a gate near here Jesus once entered the Temple precincts in triumph.

* * *

The roar of a multitude, and the urgent, victorious tramp of thousands of feet once fractured the peace of this olive garden.

The legions of the Caesars marching under the triumphal arches in Rome had been meaningless by comparison with this sudden triumph that had happened to Jesus. One instant He had seemed just one among perhaps as many as a hundred thousand pilgrims Jerusalem-bound for the Passover. The next He was singled out for adoration, became the target of shrill Alleluias. 'Blessed is he that cometh in the name of the Lord . . . hosanna to the Son of David.' And palm branches and outer clothing cushioned the four feet of the colt that bore Him onward, downward.

* * *

It takes some moments for eyes to become accustomed to the dark inside the basilica. We sat for an hour in the marbled silence, the pillared gloom becoming jewelled, suggestive of an immemorial darkness containing, at once, the embryo of the first dawn and the harbinger of the last sunset.

In the hallowed vastness knees bend as if needing no message from the brain, and eyes turn towards the Rock of His Agony. There is tension as well as peace in this place, as if the very air bears the imprint of some ancient battle.

* * *

Within twenty-four hours of the triumphal passage through the Jerusalem Gate Jesus was to be found again in the temple court. The shouts of triumph long dead upon the air, an atmosphere of gloom pervaded.[1] The voices that cried hosanna would soon find another chant. Hands would soon be bending trees to a far more sinister purpose.

A group of Greeks in the outer court came to Philip, a disciple from Bethsaida, and said: 'Sir, we should like to see Jesus.'[2] In Jerusalem for the Feast they had picked up conflicting rumours. A dead man had been raised to life not three miles distant. Jesus had overturned the tables of the money-changers, sending coinage, livestock and men in every direction. He had ridden into the city on the colt of an ass – and been hailed as if a king.

And yet . . .

They knew of a menacing conspiracy being hatched in whispers in the corridors and chambers of power.

Conflicting rumours; they came to hear the truth from Jesus Himself.

But in the light of the storm soon to break, was it truth they heard?

'The hour has come for the Son of Man to be glorified. . . . Now is the hour of judgement for this world; now shall the Prince of this world be driven out. And I shall draw all men to myself, when I am lifted up from the earth.'[3]

The disciples would catch their breath when He said 'glorified', receive His words as if the might of heaven had just been ordered to march. How strange to speak of glory with Golgotha on His mind.

Not much glory in Gethsemane; a cold, jagged rock face, the horrific struggle with the powers of darkness, the agony of betrayal.

Not much glory before Annas, Caiaphas, Herod, Pilate; mockery, scourging and a fickle crowd who had cried hosanna, shouting crucify. Condemnation, a thorn-crown and the unbearable burden of a cross.

Not much glory on Golgotha; humiliating death between two gangsters, nails square in section, raging thirst, hideous agony.

Back to Gethsemane. *Was* there glory in the Garden?

Hell pressed in upon Him. A struggle was tearing His heart in two. Scratching the rock face with extended hands, He said: 'O my Father, if it be possible . . .'[4] Nothing was inevitable. It had all been prophesied, but not predetermined. Salvation of the human race hung in the balance. A battle was being fought with the forces of darkness. Gethsemane was Christ's battleground. And the battle upstaged every battle in human history. But it was a battle won.

'. . . Nevertheless not my will but thine be done.' He would tread the winepress alone. Bear the sins of all generations to the cross, and die in the place of those who had committed and would commit them. The battle had been won, and the victory – it was glorious!

But glory before Pilate?

How little did men understand what was taking place. How little did they understand *Who* was on trial. Priests, people and rabble-rousers thought they were witnessing the trial of Jesus before the Roman governor. But only a few short hours before, they themselves, each one of them, had stood on trial before this Man. And He, knowing what they would do, had held to His decision to save them! There was glory here, glory serene and confident in the knowledge of a triumph.

But what about Calvary?

In His Gethsemane prayer He linked glory with the words: 'I have finished the work which thou gavest me to do.'[5] Man's redemption was completed, proof positive provided that there was no length to which the love of God would not go for men. The lifting up of Christ on the cross was the crumbling of the kingdom of hell. The way of escape was provided.

The glory of the cross was a continuing theme in the gospel of John. As the hoary-headed apostle neared the end of his long life he must have realized that if he was to set down on paper what he had seen and heard and felt during the three-and-a-half-year period he had spent with Jesus, he must do so now, before it was too late. As he lifted his quill pen it was as if the whole panorama of the life of Jesus passed before his eyes. For a moment he was carried away. The old evangelist broke into song, filled with joy and wonder at living for Christ in Nero's world and enthused – 'And we beheld his glory, the glory as of the only begotten of the Father. . . . He came unto his own, and his own received him not, but as many as received him, to them gave he power to become the sons of God.'[6] The glory of the cross was what the cross brought about for the sinner. The glory of the cross was the band of followers down through the centuries who, through the grace of God and the righteousness of Christ, received the power to become sons of God, those drawn by the magnetism of this death to a new life through a new birth.

* * *

Our quiet hour in the basilica ended suddenly. There was shouting outside. A pushing, shoving rabble of perhaps thirty soldiers off duty from the Lebanon tumbled in through a door to the left of the altar. They were smoking cigarettes and toting weapons. Irreverently they lolled up against the railings that surrounded the candle-lit Rock of His Agony, grinning, nudging, sniggering, exchanging significant glances.

* * *

'If it be possible, let this cup pass . . .'

He had seen the weird light of lanterns ebbing and flowing down the valley, across the hillside. At the entrance of the garden the temple guard – the flames from their torches almost engulfed by that darkest of all midnights – appeared and, with Judas in the lead, pushed in and struck out through the olive trees to make their arrest.

'. . . Nevertheless, not my will but thine be done.'

But even as they led Him away and, manacled, drove Him up the ancient Maccabean street to the house of Caiaphas, the victory had been won.

Next day the cross to which they nailed Him would appear cruel, ignominious and attended with horrors. But it would be a magnet for sinners in generations as yet unborn, and down the arches of the centuries would blaze with glory.

'King of my life, I crown Thee now,
Thine shall the glory be;
Lest I forget thy thorn-crowned brow,
Lead me to Calvary.
Lest I forget Gethsemane;
Lest I forget Thine agony;
Lest I forget Thy love for me,
Lead me to Calvary.'

1 E. G. White, *The Desire of Ages*, page 621. **2** John 12:21, NEB. **3** John 12:23, 31-33, NEB. **4** Matthew 26:39. **5** John 17:1-5. **6** John 1:10-14. See 1 John 1:1-5.

THE PALACE AND THE POTTER'S FIELD

25

Under the fierce sun of early forenoon we welcomed the shade of the trees as we made our way down the green slopes of Mount Zion.

From the city walls we had often caught sight of a beautiful basilica among the thick growth of trees. We were determined to find it. An Augustinion father, roused from his siesta, took a great key and let us into the gentle warmth of the interior of one of the most beautiful buildings we had ever entered. Consecrated in 1931 the Church of St. Peter-in-Gallicantu had been built over the excavations of the House of Caiaphas.

From the upper sanctuary, speared by sunlight from high windows, we were led down into the excavations.

The site had, we learned, been authenticated as that of the High Priest's palace by Cyril of Jerusalem as early as AD 348. Almost at the same time the courtyard adjoining had been associated with the three denials by Peter, though it had been the Crusaders who had built the first church there and given it the name Gallicantus, cock-crow. There was, however, enough Byzantine impedimenta among the excavations to indicate that they regarded it as the place of the night-time sham trial of Jesus.

We stood in a low-roofed room where hand-chosen members of the Sanhedrin would have waited, with Caiaphas, for the arrival of their Prisoner. This Caiaphas was High Priest from AD 18-36. He was son-in-law to Annas a one-time High Priest himself who, though removed from office in AD 15, managed to control things behind the scenes for many years. His five sons, one grandson and son-in-law Caiaphas were all High priests in the period AD 16-68.[1]

We climbed down into a dungeon. A 'window' above enabled the sentry to keep an eye on the Prisoner from his post. Would Jesus have been lowered into this pit for the unaccounted-for-hours of that long, dark Thursday night? Our Augustinian guide read from Psalm 88: 'My soul is full of troubles: and my life draweth nigh unto the grave. I am counted with them that go down into the pit. . . .'

There was the guard room partly restored. Two rings were visible in the second pillar; the place of scourging.

We had been joined by a reverent party of pilgrims. A woman who had not and, as we proceeded, would not speak a word, cried out and wept when she saw the scourging place . . .

. . . In imagination she was in a low-ceilinged, torch-lit chamber, crammed with soldiers and priests and tumultuous rabble with poison in their bloodstream. She felt the hysterical anger concentrate on the Prisoner upon whose face was etched, unexpurgated, the story of all the world's wickedness. Heard the quiet but bold 'I am' of the Prisoner, followed by His promise, under oath, to return in glory. Seen Caiaphas rend his robe. Heard the lashings. Then Peter's denials; Peter, after the fierce avowals of loyalty-to-the-death, intimidated by a serving wench. Then a cock crowing, and hot tears on the face of Peter. The Master led away. . . .

. . . And a nameless woman, country of origin unknown, cried out. Unseen, I left the group, paced the stairs to the sanctuary above to be alone, to think, to come to terms, to struggle with my own soul. . . .

In time the party rejoined me. From their faces I could tell that they too had sensed that they had trodden holy ground and felt the imprint of events long past left on the very air.

Outside and to the north of the basilica was an ancient stairway. It too was part of the excavations, the most important part. It represents a section of the main street of old Jerusalem linking Mount Zion (in the time of Christ 'the Upper City') with the Kidron Valley, and dates from the Maccabean period 150 years BC. Jesus and His disciples would have trodden its stones many times. Most notably they would have descended from the Upper Room to Gethsemane by this route. From Gethsemane the Temple Guard would have hustled Jesus back to the High Priest's Palace this way.

Earlier the same evening Judas would have descended

from the Upper Room to the Cheese-Makers' (Tyropoeon) Valley this way, to finalize his arrangements at the Temple for the betrayal of Jesus.

We followed his route, but, where the stairway ended, turned right down the Hinnom Valley, rather than left to the Dung Gate and Temple Mount.

In the Hinnom Valley we came upon a place known in New Testament times as Akeldama, Field of Blood.[2] With the passing of the centuries its name has changed a little. Today it is Hakk ed-Dumm, 'Purchase of Blood'.

We were on the trail of Judas once more.

The centuries have seen Judas as a man cast to play the traitor.

But the gospels portray him as a man who '*became* a traitor'.[3] He took on the role from choice.

He was chosen, like the other eleven, after Jesus had spent a night in prayer.[4] When fellow travellers forsook Jesus, Judas stood as firm as all the twelve.[5] He went out on the two-by-two preaching mission – 'Repent for the Kingdom of Heaven is at hand' – and there is no indication that he was a failure.

Only at Simon the Pharisee's Feast are we furnished with evidence of his deterioration. When Mary anointed the Master's feet, Judas said the money should have been spent on the poor. But John, at least, knew that Judas had no real concern for the poor. He had begun embezzling.[6] But was money the motive for the betrayal? A mere thirty pieces of silver?

' "The one I kiss is your man; seize him." '[7]

Judas appears at his worst here.

After a sleepless night and in the harsh light of Good Friday morning he caught a glimpse of the enormity of what he had done. 'He was seized with remorse.'[8] He braved the wrath and derision of his paymasters at the Temple. ' "I have sinned . . . for I have betrayed an innocent man," ' he told them. ' "That's your problem", they retorted.' He flung the money at their feet on the floor of the Temple. Scruples against accepting 'money paid for murder' led them to buy the Potter's Field with it, the Akeldama. It became 'a cemetery for foreigners who died in Jerusalem'.[9]

And Judas?

He never saw it.

He had fled the Temple and hanged himself.

* * *

Peter denied his Lord. Judas betrayed Him.

When Jesus called Simon He saw his potential and called him Peter, Rock-Man. He saw potential in Judas too. But Judas changed course.

The most important fact about the story of Judas is that it need not have ended as it did.

In the final hours it was not only Judas who failed his Lord. In Gethsemane they all 'forsook him, and fled'.[10] Peter denied Him three times under the taunts of a serving wench.

But the disciples, and specifically Peter, were recommissioned by the Risen Lord.

There is much that is commendable about the confession of Judas. There was no attempt to shift blame, to wash his hands like Pilate.

The ultimate tragedy of the Judas story is not the betrayal, *but what he failed to do when the moment of truth came upon him.*

* * *

Both Peter and Judas were Hakk ed-Dumm, 'the Purchase of Blood'.

Judas *could* have asked forgiveness from the Man on the central cross – and received it.

Instead he hanged himself.

We have betrayed our Lord.

We have denied our Lord.

At the moment of truth may we not succumb to despair like Judas, but fall at the feet of the Master like Peter.

1 F. F. Bruce, *The Real Jesus*, page 37. **2** Acts 1:19. **3** Luke 6:16, NIV. **4** Luke 6:12, 13. **5** John 6:64-71. **6** John 12:1-8. **7** Matthew 26:48, NEB. **8** Matthew 27:3, NEB. **9** Matthew 27:3-10, TLB. **10** Matthew 26:56.

A PAVEMENT, A DREAM, A CROSS AND A CROWN

26

Pontius Pilate was not his name. He was born Lucius Pontius. His father, Marcus, fought so well for the legions of Rome that he was decorated. He received the coveted Pilum. And the Pilum was an honour so resplendent that it demanded a permanent memorial: a change of name. Hence, Pilate.

Lucius Pontius Pilate followed in his father's footsteps. He fought in the legions, and in the Germanic campaigns was brought to the notice of the Emperor, Tiberius. He returned to Rome in search of political office. Instead he found and fell in love with Claudia, granddaughter of the late Emperor Augustus, and hence a member of the Imperial family.

Rome knew how to celebrate a marriage, and celebrated the marriage of Lucius and Claudia with pomp, pageantry and dancing in the streets. In the course of the celebrations a parchment arrived from Tiberius. The Emperor's wedding present was the governorship of Judea – with orders to sail immediately. But the orders included an unusual departure from protocol; Claudia was allowed to accompany her governor-husband to his post of duty.

* * *

Of Roman Caesarea on the coast, from where Pilate governed this turbulent, frontier province, there is little remaining. And most of that is under an unnaturally coloured sea, toxic with effluent pumped out by nearby chemical works. An inscription discovered among the ruins bears his name.

Pilate and Claudia resided in Jerusalem's Antonia Fortress for the duration of the great feasts. At such times it was advisable for the governor to be on hand in case of insurrection. Even today as Passover time approaches and both Jews and Christians make preparation for their coincident religious festivals there is a similar build-up of tension.

Christian preparations centre on the Via Dolorosa, which passes over the site of the Antonia Fortress. Here there is the arch of Ecce Homo. Beside it, easy to overlook, is the doorway to the Convent of the Sisters of Zion.

Inside, the Sisters handed us over to a young American guide. He showed us round the excavations of the fort. Built by Herod the Great twenty years BC it had, he said, been named after Mark Anthony. In coming down the flight of steps from the Convent, we had descended twenty centuries. Here were two huge cisterns which had supplied the garrisons with water. There was a triple triumphal arch – the *original* arch of Ecce Homo. Could Jesus have passed through it on the *original* Way of Sorrows?

But, most important, there was the pavement, the Lithostratos, the courtyard outside the Praetorium gates. 'Pilate . . . brought Jesus forth, and sat down in the judgement seat in the place that is called the Pavement, but in the Hebrew, Gabbatha.'[1]

We were standing on the huge paving stones of an old Roman street. There were great slabs of limestone and granite, rutted with grooves worn by chariot wheels and lacquered smooth by a myriad bare feet, long stilled. Engraved in the stones were the games played by Roman guards, perhaps waiting for a trial to end and a crucifixion to begin; knucklebones, the Game of the King.

Time raced backwards.

* * *

The paving stones are there. Ahead is the Gate of the Praetorium. An unruly crowd has assembled in the chill before the Friday dawn. The jostling crowd is in the process of becoming a seething mob. They are being spurred on, drummed up – and bought. Derisive voices snarl in the darkness.

At the front of the mêlée are the convulsive figures of two men, arms upraised, voices hoarse with shrieking. The elderly, once majestic figure of Annas – the tireless old boss of Jerusalem; and Caiaphas, his torn blue robe trailing in the dust. The ill-used Prisoner, bruised and bleeding, shivers in the chill of the morning outside the still-closed gates.

Blindfolded, buffeted back and forth, His hands tied before Him, He has dignity still.

The first yellow streaks appear in the eastern sky.

There is the rumble of wheels, the screech of hinges, and the Praetorium gates fall inward.

Pilate is revealed in his chair of ivory on a high platform.

* * *

Josephus Flavius and Philo Judaeus give long, though biased accounts of this governor of Judea.

He had a cynical contempt for the Jewish race, perched on the edge of the world and yet laying claim to some innate superiority based on their religion. On his first arrival at Jerusalem in AD 26 he had deliberately ended the Roman practice of deferring to Jewish scruples on graven images. Under cover of darkness he had moved his troops in and, the following morning, the city had woken up to Imperial standards, topped by the eagle and the Imperial image on public buildings and on the city walls. There had been uproar and frantic deputations from the ruling classes. He had been outmanoeuvred and forced to remove the standards.

He had financed the building of an aqueduct with gold from the Temple treasury. The storm had broken during a Passover week. Pilate had ordered a blood bath.

Now, faced by a delirious mob and a serene Christ, he knew that a complaint against him was on its way to Tiberius from the Samaritans. He feared lest he should be called to account for his oppressions and extortions.

* * *

The exchanges begin. 'Art thou the King of the Jews? . . . What is truth? . . . Answerest thou nothing?'

The air is rent by an iterative chant.

'We have no king but Caesar! Crucify Him! Crucify Him!'

Jewish leaders are angry. Is Pilate opening a fresh trial?

The yellowish streaks in the eastern sky expand and become orange, and the world grows lighter. The shadows on the Prisoner's visage fall away. The marks of anguish are there.

And now He stands before Pilate.

'What shall I do then with Jesus?' the governor asks. 'I find no fault with Him! What evil hath He done?'

'Crucify Him! Crucify Him! Release unto us Barabbas!' demand the inflamed mob. Pilate ponders the irony. They are wanting to set an insurgent free – and convict the preacher of non-resistance of insurgency!

Jesus continues serene and silent. Pilate barks enraged –

'Speakest Thou not unto me? Knowest Thou not that I have power to crucify Thee, and have power to release Thee?'

The Man, he is thinking, can't know what crucifixion means, else He'd talk! The scourging, the flagellum, the nails through the hands and the feet, the horrible raging thirst, flies buzzing and crawling endlessly . . .

* * *

The trial is at its height.

The air is electric.

The eyes of the crowd bulge. Voices screech in hysteria. The chief priests and the scribes act like men possessed.

It is at this point that a tribune approaches Pilate with a message on a silver tray. The message is from Claudia. *At the height of the trial, and Claudia is writing messages!*

'His wife sent unto him, saying, Have thou nothing to do with that just man: for I have suffered many things this day in a dream because of him.'[2]

That just Man. Pilate reflects. In most prisoners there would have been the fierce courage of fanaticism; but there is no fanaticism in Christ. In most prisoners there would have been that meanness which will do anything to escape death; but he can see nothing of this in Jesus. In Him is an unusual gentleness and humility combined with majestic dignity.

He *will* spare this just Man if he can do so without endangering himself.

And there is a pause in the proceedings.

Perhaps a pause placed there for Pilate's own benefit – *and by God Himself.*

Pilate's last chance.

It is the fifth year of Pilate's marriage to Claudia, and he has never known her to act like this. At the height of a sensitive trial to act on the impulse of a daytime dream. And to adopt so imperious a tone; *'Have thou nothing to do . . .'* An authoritative message from a wife to a husband, and he a governor. She must warn her husband before there is blood on his hands that cataracts of water can never wash away.

'If anything beneath the moon may be thought to be exempt from law, and to be the creature of pure chance, surely it is a dream', says Charles Haddon Spurgeon. 'True, there were in old times dreams in which God spake to men prophetically; but ordinarily they are the carnival of thought, a maze of mental states, a dance of disorder . . . dreams are the most disorderly of phenomena, and yet it seems they may be ordered of the Lord . . .'

And the Romans have a superstition that morning dreams are true.

* * *

Her husband had arisen early and left the bed-chamber in haste. Claudia slept on into the daylight. The chanting of the mob that shuddered the bowel and made arms tingle, penetrated her subconscious.

* * *

And in her daytime vision, ordered of the Lord, *what did she see?*

That night when the stars sang, heaven drew nigh to earth – and a baby was born in Bethlehem's stable?

A boy struggling to manhood in the have-not street of a mean town?

The sun-warmed days by the inland sea? Men and women among the nets on the shingle wrapped in His words?

Capernaum, Bethsaida, Jericho – the streets of Zion itself in the heat of the day, and a tall, purposeful figure quietly laying hands upon the maimed and the sick, making men whole? The same man amid the scabrous lepers in their sealed-off valleys of misery, right in the middle of them, touching the untouchable, watching the healthy skin return, and with it smiles and laughter and hopes for the future?

The mountains at Gadara; the daylight of reason let into dim, shuttered minds?

The Pool of Siloam; sight returning so that eyes could glimpse light and beauty and truth again?

The valley beyond Bethany; the Voice of command that made devils convulse and death release its claimed victim?

The west-facing slopes of the Mount of Olives; sharp-worded denunciations of the ecclesiastical bosses? Then apocalyptic echoes of a future in which Jerusalem must fall – and, at length, thrones and kingdoms be dashed in pieces, and the vault of heaven full-brilliant with angels . . . ?

. . . And in Claudia's subconscious roared the mob on the Lithostratos, at the Gate of the Praetorium; howling, braying, thundering. . . . '*I have suffered much* in a dream because of Him . . . .'

* * *

. . . Did she see the crown made of the long-thorned briar, crushed savagely down on the brow of the Prisoner? . . . The flagellum, the whip tipped with nails and scraps of bones, wielded by soldiers with arms like shot-putters? . . .

. . . Her husband vascillating, convinced of the innocence of the Prisoner but 'willing to content the people' . . . . 'If thou let this man go, thou art not Caesar's friend . . . .'[3] A man with legions at his back, afraid of a Jewish mob . . . ?

Then, with a letter in his hand, the condemnation.

. . . Did the horror of sending an innocent man to a hideous death seize Claudia in her trance? . . . The baulk of timber about seven or eight feet long borne on the lacerated back of the Prisoner to the place of execution, driven on by blows from the flat of the sword . . . . At the place of execution, the Prisoner felled, the baulk of timber thrust beneath his neck . . . arms gripped while heavy iron nails are hammered through the forward fold of the wrist . . . the entire hideous instrument of torture and execution, with the Prisoner upon it – *this* Prisoner, this King of Truth, not of this world – hoisted in the air and savagely jolted down into the place prepared for it . . . .

. . . The feet nailed, one nail driven between the metatarsal bones of the two crossed insteps . . . .

. . . intense, insupportable agony caused by the incomplete severing of the median nerves by the nails through the wrists, vibrating through the arm to explode in the brain at every moment . . . endlessly twisting, seeking relief from this onslaught on the senses . . .

. . . laboured breath gasp by gasp, raging thirst . . . .

. . . Did Claudia see Him there, spittle upon His beard, the upper face red from the thorn-crown? Did she look into the faces of the crowd? Upturned faces, registering hatred? Did she recognize her own among them?

And Claudia; did she understand what it all meant? *His* hands pierced for the wrong things *our* hands have done. *His* feet spiked for the wrong paths *our* feet have trod. *His* brow thorn-crushed for the wrong thoughts *our* minds have harboured. *His* heart broken for the wrong things *our* hearts have loved. *His* side riven to prove once and for all that the way to God's heart is wide open.

And when, with a loud voice, He said, *'It is finished'*, did she understand that it was a finished redemption? That the price of sin had been paid? That the destructive power of sin had been broken? That through the pardoning blood of Christ a man might stand before God *as though he had never sinned*? Did she understand that God's love for the world had been shown to have no limit? That He so loved the world that He was giving His only begotten Son? That whosoever believeth on Him shall not perish but have everlasting life? And that freedom from the thrall and guilt of sin, pardon, peace, justification, and eternal life were all decided here? The choice *ours?*

Did she see the band of followers down through the misty centuries of the future . . . the martyrs, the persecuted, the heroes of His Gospel dedicate life and suffer death for His great Cause?

Did she see an end-time 'remnant of the faithful' who had 'come out of great tribulation' and had washed their robes and 'made them white in the blood of the Lamb'?[4] Did she hear a Voice say of the beleagued victorious, 'Here is the patience of the saints; here are they that keep the commandments of God, and the faith of Jesus'?[5]

And at the end of all things, did she see 'a great multitude, which no man could number, of all nations, and kindreds, and people, and tongues' standing before the throne and before the Lamb clothed with white robes, and palms in their hands, as the Revelator saw in vision: those washed in the blood of the Lamb and transformed by His power and covered by His righteousness?[6]

At the end of Claudia's vision, surely, and to her amazement, she would recognize the thorn-crowned Prisoner – in a new guise. That scene in the vaulted skies. And, in the midst, no longer 'the Prisoner' but the King of kings.

Amid an atomic hailstorm on a day when the sky rained fire, the Prisoner with nail-pierced hands outstretched is drawing His followers into a blaze of glory stretched from sky to sky.

The crucifiers have been resurrected and look on. Poor, weak Pilate, her husband, is among them.[7] 'And the kings of the earth, and the great men, and the rich men, and the chief captains, and the mighty men, and every bondman, and every free man, hid themselves in the dens and the rocks of the mountains; and said to the mountains and rocks, Fall on us, and hide us from the face of him that sitteth on the throne, and from the wrath of the Lamb: for the great day of his wrath is come; and who shall be able to stand?'[8]

Again she sees the company of the redeemed, a numberless throng. Does she recognize her own face among the redeemed standing on a sea of glass shot through with fire, and singing the glories of the Prisoner whom even now her husband is sending to crucifixion?

* * *

Claudia's vision was Pilate's divine ultimatum. It went unheeded. After a time he was summoned to Rome to answer the charge brought against him by the Samaritans. Claudia and Pilate ended their days in Gaul. Weary of his misfortunes, Pilate terminated his own life, it was said. The evidence suggests that Claudia at her life's end was a devout follower of the Prisoner with the thorn-crown and nail-pierced hands.

'*What shall I do then with Jesus?*' Pilate had asked. He had accepted the reply, 'Let Him be crucified.'

But Claudia, she crowned Him; crowned Him King of her life.

Pilate's question echoes through the arches of the ages, echoes even in *our* ears.

We must answer that question; it is the most important we will ever be asked.

By way of answer we may either crucify Him as Pilate did, or crown Him as Claudia did.

* * *

As the unnatural darkness lifted, the words that sounded over the confusion were, 'It is finished.'

'Never has evil been so ruthlessly exposed as on Calvary; nowhere can God's love more prefectly be seen. Nothing remains to be done to make possible man's return to God. God can do no more. That is why the cross is a judgement – "Now is the judgement of this world" – refused, it is the end of hope. That is why the cross redeems – accepted, it is the end of all endeavour to save ourselves. It is accomplished.'[9] *It is* finished.

1 John 19:13. See F. F. Bruce, *The Real Jesus*, page 105. **2** Matthew 27:19. **3** John 19:12. **4** Revelation 7:14. **5** Revelation 14:12. **6** Revelation 7:9-13. **7** Revelation 1:7. **8** Revelation 6:15-17. **9** R. E. O. White, *The Stranger of Galilee*, page 110.

VIA DOLOROSA

27

Once, and only once, we followed the Procession of the Cross along the Via Dolorosa.

A crowd of thousands assembled at the Church of St. Anne by the arched ruins of the once magnificent Pools of Bethesda. It seemed that every nationality from all five continents in both hemispheres had its representatives among us.

The man carrying the cross emerged from Ecce Homo with three priests in attendance, Latin, Orthodox and Protestant. The multitude surged forward in that narrow, terraced walkway and enclosed them on all sides. As we stumbled forward we struggled to remain within sight of the shoulder-borne cross and within earshot of the three priests who at intervals stopped and read, the Protestant in English.

Not infrequently Good Friday Jerusalem skies are black and pregnant with thunder. Pilgrims have been drenched under heavens furious with sobbing rain. But the day we followed the cross the Way of Sorrows was dappled in Easter sunshine.

The Arabs whose shops we passed, for once, did not press their wares; olive wood souvenirs, leatherwork, clocks and Coca Cola. But from Middle Eastern smells – essence of decay, new leather, fruit in various stages of overripeness, cooking, bad drains – there was no escape.

As we clambered up the terraced street the Way was completely arched over. The whining music from the bazaars became more difficult to ignore.

At one station of the cross, the priests' voices were rendered inaudible by the volume of the muezzin.

As we neared the top of the terraced street which had begun at St. Stephen's Gate, our advanced party, including the cross-bearer, suddenly fell back. A number lost their footing. Round the corner strode, purposefully and at some speed, a conversation-absorbed conflux of Jews. Most of them were clean-shaven young yeshiva (religious academy) students in broad-brimmed hats. Others were bearded Hasidim in long black overcoats with curled sidelocks dangling from beneath their fedoras. 'Those were the fighting Orthodox', a Swedish professor of politics staying at the hospice would tell me that evening. 'In their Eretz Israel – frontiered as in the Old Testament – there is no room for Christian or Muslim devotion. Many of them live among the decayed buildings and billowing wash-lines of the Mea She'arim. The dark-clothed Hasidim are a Jewish sect originally founded in eighteenth-century Poland in mystical rebellion against the spiritual and academic authority of their Rabbinic leaders. . . .'

But 'fighting Orthodox' or no, they simply ignored the presence of the thousands of Christians, and passed on down. A more typical Ashkenazi, who had seen it all, apologized for them: 'They seem to invite anti-semitism', he said. 'They deliberately antagonize the goyim. . . .'

The Via Dolorosa came to a T-junction and, indicated by an ancient blue ceramic embedded in the wall, took a sharp left. To the right was the widening terraced way to the Damascus Gate. Leftwards we headed through an arched-over bazaar packed and overhung with every kind of merchandise. Narrow, stepped alleys opened up on either hand revealing unspeakable squalor. In one a blind Palestinian with a purple birthmark across his face – we had seen him many times before begging inside the New Gate – sat with outstretched hands. Behind him, in doorways littered with refuse, urchins played. Washing hung from drooping lines just below the incongruous TV aerials.

In a neighbouring alley there was, apparently, a station of the cross, for the priests stopped for readings. Wedged in the main bazaar we breathed in to allow a heavily laden mule, driven by a small boy, to pass on its way to the Damascus Gate. Alone in these dense, airless walkways of Old Jerusalem we felt threatened and compelled to hurry. With strength in numbers we were content to saunter on. Through imposing archways we saw the wide Muristan bazaar – and beyond it the Muristan Square and fountain. In these environs medieval pilgrims from Western Europe had found their accommodation.

Then the sunlit square of the Church of the Holy Sepulchre burst upon us. As we entered the gate a man said, 'Crown of thorns, buy here!'

With their backs to the sun the mighty throng of pilgrims entered the dank, dark depths of the ancient church. Surrounded by censers hanging from chains which reached into the darkness above: a marble slab where they said His body had been nailed to the instrument of execution. Moving with the multitude we clambered up steps to what they called Calvary, a cavern forested with candlesticks and chain-hung censers. In the dim light, over the hundreds of heads, we could still make out the shape of the cross. But the almost inaudible prayers and readings sounded like muttered incantations.

The multitude dispersed.

The man with the cross was gone.

We were left alone to make sense of the conflicting impressions, to analyse the powerful emotions that possessed us. Emptiness, disappointment, disillusionment. Did the Church of the Holy Sepulchre strike all pilgrims this way?

* * *

Eighteen months before, we had embarked upon an adventure, a quest. In common with twenty centuries of pilgrims we had come in search – of Jesus Christ. The sound of *His* footfall. The imprint of *His* presence. In the course of the journey we had often felt that the trail was warm.

Quiet moments by Galilee.

Under the gushing waterfall at Caesarea Philippi.

In the Garden of Gethsemane.

In the house of Caiaphas.

On the massive flagstones of the Lithostratos where He stood before Pilate.

And, as if by a natural progression, our quest had led us to the Way of Sorrows. In that Good Friday throng we had learned much about the hard-bitter passions so close to the surface in that turbulent land. We had inhaled the stench of its social unrest and its cynical commercialism. But the quest for

Christ had gone cold where the trail should have been warmest. Stone cold.

The crowds gone, we began to wander, unguided, around the warren of shrines and alcoves in the Church of the Holy Sepulchre. Everywhere was the scent of incense. It was overpowering. We went to the sepulchre itself in the centre of a domed basilica. It was encased in mahogany, ancient and ornately carved. An Eastern Orthodox priest knelt and crossed himself many times before the marbled slab which covered the stone inside the sepulchre.

In only one place was there a stone surface reminiscent of the rock-hewn tomb prepared for Joseph of Arimathea. It was at the rear of the sepulchre. A second spade-bearded priest crouched by the side of it. He beckoned us. It seemed almost indecent. Beside him was a heap of Deutsche marks, dollars and pounds sterling. He managed to convey the idea that, in exchange for touching the stone, payment would be required. The only words he uttered, hand outstretched, were 'Shekel? Shekel?'

Back to Calvary. An Orthodox priest sat silently to the left of the altar. To the right a nun knelt in rapt admiration at a statuette of the Blessed Virgin encased in glass. A helpful Latin priest took me by the arm. We had no languages in common. Together we knelt below the altar, and he took my right hand and placed it through a brass ring on the floor. Beneath the brass ring I felt cold rock. Later, in a guide book, I read that it was here that the cross was inserted into the rock face.

Here was a place of death, a celebration of death, a mausoleum to a dead Messiah. That was my impression then, as it is now. Am I over-reacting? The place bespoke death and mourning; a Christ who was still dead, not One who lived and reigned and made intercession for us at the right hand of God. The Christ of this place was – or so it seemed, and seems, to me – a hideous gothic figure eternally on a cross, or a wasted corpse ministered to by hooded priests. I can only hope that others may receive a more positive experience.

We fled the church. And, for that day at any rate, the city. We were relieved to be free of it.

* * *

Following her destruction in AD 70, Jerusalem lay in ruins until AD 130. Any Christians who returned to clamber over its heaps of masonry would have had difficulty identifying with any certainty the exact spot where Jesus was crucified or the tomb where His body had lain. In AD 130 Jerusalem, for sixty years no more than the camp of the Tenth Legion, was visited by the Emperor Hadrian. He ordered that the site be cleared, and a brand new Roman city built. This city of columns, colonnades, forums, Roman villas and heathen temples was called Ælia Capitolina. Though its walls followed the old Jewish ramparts, there was no further resemblance to the Herodian city. Nevertheless, the tradition had developed by the time of St. Helena's visit – when, ruled by her son Constantine, the empire was nominally Christian – that Hadrian's Temple of Venus had been built over the site of Calvary. Hence in AD 336 the heathen temple was ordered to be demolished and replaced by a Christian church. Over the centuries this building was burned repeatedly and often remained in ruins for many years at a time. The present Church of the Holy Sepulchre, actually a collection of churches squabbled over by the Orthodox, Catholic, Coptic and Abyssinian Churches – among others – began to develop into its present inelegant shape at the time of the Crusades.

* * *

On the day following the Pilgrimage of the Cross, Shabat, we walked around the top of Jerusalem's walls, beginning at the Jaffa Gate. At the Damascus Gate it was necessary to descend. Quite by accident we stumbled into Hadrian's Jerusalem, now underneath the other Jerusalems which have superseded it.

We had taken the narrow stone staircase by mistake. It led us well below the level of the present Damascus Gate – to the excavations beneath. Here we found the double northern gate completed by Hadrian's masons around AD 135. It was brought to our attention that much of this gate was built from Herodian stone. Archaeologists have drawn the conclusion that this northern entrance to Hadrian's city was built in place of the ruined structure of an Herodian gate. A number of those who had examined the evidence concluded that the first structure to stand on this site was in fact the Gate Ganeth. And it has always been asserted that it was through the Gate Ganeth that Jesus carried His cross to the place of execution beyond the city walls.

In the week that followed we were to examine more of Hadrian's Ælia Capitolina. In the Roman plan of the city a street extended from this northern gate to a point very near to what is now the Zion Gate. So much of this street has been excavated that it has been possible, beneath the level of present-day Jerusalem, to reconstruct a whole precinct of Roman buildings. This precinct, The Cardo, has become a busy thoroughfare, reconstructed Roman buildings converted into shops by enterprising Israelis.

This was exciting. But even more exciting to us was the re-configuration of the Way of the Cross made necessary by the discovery of the probable site of the Gate Ganeth – to the north, not the west of the city as formerly assumed. From this northern gate – in Hadrian's time, as Herod's, as now – the Great Road strikes north to Shekem (Nablus), Samaria and, ultimately, Damascus.

Not 200 yards from this northern gate – near the Great Road and well within sight of the city walls, a typical site for Roman crucifixions – is an ancient place of execution.[1] It is called Skull Hill and represents the northernmost outcrop of Mount Moriah, Temple Mount being its southernmost outcrop. A team of American archaeologists have made an interesting case for the authenticity of this site as that of the crucifixion of Jesus, and, linked with it, the authenticity of the Garden Tomb nearby. The arguments they use to raise questions with regard to the Latin Calvary are based on its nearness to Herod's palace (the Citadel by the Jaffa Gate incorporates the base of one of its towers) and significant evidence that, though outside the walled city until a little after the crucifixion, the Church of the Holy Sepulchre would have been in the centre of an opulent suburb thick with the substantial villas of wealthy Jews during the period of Jesus' ministry.

Which, if either, is the 'authentic site' of the crucifixion and resurrection of Jesus, we cannot be sure. Nor is it particularly important that we should be sure. The crucifixion and resurrection have significance for our lives. Exactly where they happened does not.

But at the Church of the Holy Sepulchre we felt we had caught the breath of Christianity-gone-wrong. We had been profoundly shocked by the way in which Christianity's Founder and His Gospel had been misrepresented, lost in a timeless gloaming in which His truth fused with heathenism and superstitious practice.

What should have brought us face to face with the sublimely simple, simply sublime Gospel of Jesus Christ had, instead, served to remind us of the dire warnings of perils ahead uttered by New Testament writers as the first soldiers of the cross perished at their posts.

Jesus had warned of false prophets who would lead many astray. When the apostle John came to write his three letters he was concerned to point out that the peril for the present, as for the future, was not persecution but seduction; not attack from without but corruption from within. Jude, in verse 3 of his letter, exhorts the faithful 'earnestly to contend for the faith which was once delivered to the saints'. The menace to Christ's Church foreseen by Paul in his letters and John in the book of Revelation – both reflecting the Old Testament prophecies of Daniel – was a menace primarily religious, only secondarily political. Its impact would be to corrupt the main body of the Church, and harass and persecute the minority faithful to Christ's Gospel.

1 Evidence of the authenticity of Skull Hill and the Garden Tomb, and doubts with regard to the authenticity of the siting of the Latin Calvary, are drawn from Dr. William McBirnie's book, based on twenty years of research undertaken with a team of specialists, *The Search for the Authentic Tomb of Jesus*, first published in 1975.

‘THERE WAS A GARDEN . . .’

28

‘Joseph of Arimathea . . . besought Pilate that he might take away the body of Jesus: and Pilate gave him leave. He came therefore, and took the body of Jesus. . . . Now in the place where he was crucified there was a garden; and in the garden a new sepulchre, wherein was never man yet laid. There laid they Jesus . . . for the sepulchre was nigh at hand.’[1]

* * *

The old city is at its noisiest and its wickedest in the area inside the Damascus Gate. It is a teeming, touting, elbow-tugging, shoving-and-pushing, hurly-burly. Arabs, Armenians and Sephardic Jews peddle an infinite variety of merchandise.

But a few hundred yards north of the Gate is a place of peace, where pomegranates grow on trees and brightly coloured flowers bloom everywhere. At one end of the garden is a sinister, skull-shaped hill, an ancient place of execution.

At the other extremity is an empty tomb. It is the rock-hewn tomb of a rich man, not a cave. Outside, there is a groove where once a mighty stone was moved into position.

We have visited that Easter garden with its empty tomb scores of times. But we shall never forget the first time. With a group of Canadians and Americans we filed slowly in and out of the tomb, three hundred or so of us, singing softly, ‘There in the grave He lay, Jesus my Saviour; waiting the coming day, Jesus my Lord. Up from the grave He arose . . .’

We stood outside the tomb for hours looking on, choking on our words.

A woman with crippled legs was carried into the tomb – and was carried out weeping and beaming at the same time.

A silver-haired septuagenarian from Kent burst out of the tomb with joy on her honest face and in her voice as she echoed the words of the angel to Mary, ‘He is not here. He is risen!’

A young man, only recently a Christian, from Papua New Guinea, eyes glistening, face beaming, body trembling, said: 'I shall go home and tell everyone that the tomb of Jesus Christ is empty!'

George Vandeman has said: 'Other great religions worship at the tombs of their founders. But there isn't a shrine in the world that claims one bone of the body of Christ. He left death eternally behind that day – and left an empty tomb as a witness. A Roman seal couldn't hold Him there. Roman executioners couldn't keep Him there. Mountains piled on mountains would not have been enough.'

Bill White, a Church of England minister whose work involves having oversight of the garden, said: 'When they put the Lord there He was very, very dead. And if anyone knew how to make sure that a man was very, very dead it was the Romans! But on the first light of Sunday morning He was very much alive!'

We were fascinated by this man who had, himself, suffered a stroke and a great deal of personal tragedy. Through repeated visits we have become firm friends.

'Spaces in the tomb were originally chiselled out for two persons, a man and his wife', he once told me. 'But only one of the places was ever occupied. There is evidence of last-minute chiselling to accommodate the frame of a much larger corpse – taller, broader shouldered. Clearly, not the one for whom the tomb was intended. The occupying corpse would have been five feet eleven inches in height. It is interesting that the Turin Shroud has on it the negative image of a thorn-crowned, crucified man of exactly this height . . .'

Here he checked himself.

'But that is not the important thing', he said. 'The real proof of the risen Christ is not to be found in relics or shrines or parchments or sacred places. It is to be found in His accessibility – availability – now, to you and to me. "He is not here for He is risen." '

Christ is risen!

But we had heard the sound of His footfall as He stepped from death into life.

We had seen the imprint of His feet.

We had heard the sound of His voice saying, 'Mary.'

We had felt the immediacy of His presence.

Nowhere in all that land was His presence closer than in that garden where there was an empty tomb.

* * *

The first Christians believed that Jesus rose because they met Him. And the acid test of the resurrection is still personal encounter. 'We have seen the Lord', they said.[2]

'He was seen of James';[3] James, His brother.

On an evening-road of sadness – Jerusalem to Emmaus – He joined two of His disciples. Over a meal at home they, at last, recognized their Guest. Then wasted no time in making the return journey. Back in Jerusalem they reported to the eleven and discovered, 'The Lord is risen indeed, and hath appeared to Simon.'[4]

Mary had been in the garden alone, Sunday morning, first light. Through blinding tears she knew Him only when He spoke her name.[5]

Saul, who became Paul, encountered the risen Christ on the way to extirpate Christianity in Damascus. His resistance crumbled on the instant of encounter.[6]

The risen Lord appeared to various groups at different times before the ascension, on one occasion to five hundred, most of whom were still alive to testify twenty years later.[7]

The fact and power of the resurrection launched 'a winged thunderbolt of everlasting enthusiasm' (G. K. Chesterton). From Jerusalem, an intensely heated centre of burning zeal, a vast field of lava was thrown out to the limits of the Roman world. But the men at the centre of all this had fled from Gethsemane! One had denied his Lord with oaths! All had spent the period between crucifixion and resurrection holed up behind closed doors, bolted and barred!

But the very same men were preaching the resurrection before vast crowds converting thousands. The empty tomb served as a visual aid to their preaching: a fact, there, present, accessible, proof and no doubt.

The fact is, however, that the resurrection had caught these men completely unprepared. *Afterwards* they recalled His promises. But at the time, far from inventing the resurrection, they themselves, against their inclinations, had to be persuaded that it was a fact.

Fear gripped everyone. That is why the first words of the Easter angels were ' "Do not be afraid." ' They 'hurried away from the tomb afraid', 'Trembling and bewildered . . . fled from the tomb', 'In their fright . . . bowed down', 'They were startled and frightened, thinking they saw a ghost.' ' "Why are you troubled," Jesus asked with some sternness, "and why do doubts rise in your minds?" '[8]

Fear of the Jews kept the doors locked. Fear of the supernatural kept their minds locked. Understandable, of course, but there would be no point inventing it. They were too scared to do any 'wishful thinking'. 'They still did not believe it because of joy and amazement.'[9] Even when the facts were irrefutable they hardly dared believe; the only activities which had occupied their hands and minds since the crucifixion were those connected with embalming the dead.

The women – Salome, Mary of Magdala and Mary the mother of James – had been left to bear the brunt of Good Friday's tragedy. They watched at a distance as Joseph of Arimathea and Nicodemus took the corpse down from the cross, laid it in the rock-hewn tomb which was then secured by a great stone rolled over its entrance, a seal and a watch of soldiers.

Before the first light of Sunday morning the three women were hurrying through the narrow, darkened streets of the lower city. In their hands were the impedimenta of embalming. As they made for the garden tomb, wraiths of mist ashen about the feet, they were worried as to how they would roll away the stone 'which was very large'.[10] These women did not expect a resurrection. Far from it. Their analysis of what they saw was practical, clinical, and common sense: ' "They have taken the Lord out of the tomb." '[11] Two on the road to Emmaus were aware of the women's testimony and dismissed it with the words: ' "Him they did not see." '[12]

Peter left the tomb 'wondering to himself what had happened';[13] The others 'did not understand from Scripture that Jesus had to rise from the dead'. 'They did not believe the women, because their words seemed to them like nonsense.'[14] Even after Christ's final appearance 'some doubted'.[15]

Eventually Jesus Himself 'rebuked them for their lack of faith and their stubborn refusal to believe'.[16] There is no picture here of imagination gone wild creating a glowing picture of victory to satisfy pious hope. To sceptical moods, exalted visions do not come. Nor do men seeking to deceive others confess to sadness, despair, fear, unbelief, astonishment.[17]

Of course, faith came at last. Then hope, expanding. Then limitless joy. Finally readiness to die rather than deny.

Out of crushed, beaten-down men, grew the most powerful force known to history. The very violence of Rome's reaction to this 'winged thunderbolt' is evidence that the empire had felt its power at her very foundation.

Truth outstrips invention. *They* said they had seen the risen Christ. Their lives confirmed their words; and their violent, grisly deaths upheld the testimony of their lives.

Fidelity to Jesus Christ has never been the soft option. The cost has always been high. But countless thousands have paid it.

A motiveless fraud could not have sustained the Church for 2,000 years through attack, hostility and denial.

* * *

Before the sun had risen far over the dark ridges of the mountains of Moab and Ammon that Sunday morning the news was spreading that Jesus Christ was risen! That the grave had given up its victory and that the living Son of the living God, a dead Man an hour ago, had, in the lonely morning, been seen and spoken to! The Holy One was not suffered to see corruption but, according to the prophecy, on the third day was raised up!

The Lord is risen indeed!

1 John 19:38-42. **2** John 20:25. **3** 1 Corinthians 15:7. **4** Luke 24:12-34. **5** Mark 16:9-11; John 20:10-17. **6** Acts 9:1-6. **7** 1 Corinthians 15:6. **8** Matthew 28:5, 8; Mark 16:5, 6, 8; Luke 24:4, 5, 37-39; see also John 20:13, NIV. **9** Luke 24:41, NIV. **10** Mark 16:1-4, NIV. **11** John 20:2, NIV. **12** Luke 24:22-24, NIV. **13** Luke 24:12, NIV. **14** John 20:9; Luke 24:11, NIV. **15** Matthew 28:17, NIV. **16** Mark 16:14, NIV. **17** R. E. O. White, *Stranger of Galilee*, page 158.

TO RISE AGAIN

29

Whenever we stand at the mouth of the empty tomb it moves us strangely.

On the first occasion we visited the Garden we thought: 'It is the Englishman's Calvary.' But we became aware of a variety of language groups and nationalities there.

On the second visit we thought: 'It is the Protestant's Calvary.' But there were nuns and spade-bearded Eastern monks there – and soldiers, American blacks from the United Nations peace-keeping force in the Lebanon.

On the third and on subsequent visits we have wondered whether the resurrection did in fact take place there. The pulse races a little, small hairs bristle, words are caught in the throat.

Whether in this or in another garden very like it, death died at the birth of that first Easter day. That morning it surrendered dominion, was led captive and humbled, made, as it were, a shadow to flee before a Light shining in the darkness.

The destruction of death and him that hath the power of death, sin and Satan, was made certain that morning of Resurrection.

The colourful trees and flowering shrubs of the Garden provide a good ambience for contemplation of the significance of the resurrection of Jesus.

We have often discussed it with the chaplain, the Revd. Bill White. He has given me a copy of his book, *The Thing Incredible*. He has written his name on it, and a Bible verse, Philippians 3:10. *'That I may know him, and the power of his resurrection, and the fellowship of his sufferings, being made conformable unto his death.'*

Here the significance of the resurrection is summarized. The three central acts of Christianity are here celebrated in the confines of one verse: His death – *our* death, our sins, our self-life dying with Him; His burial – the burial of *our* sins, lost in the fathomless sea of God's forgetfulness; His resurrection – *our* resurrection, a resurrection to a new, abundant life that knows the peace, the joy and the power of the risen Lord – the Risen Life.

The guilt of sin is left behind at the cross. It is buried, never to be exhumed – unless *we* exhume it.

In the Risen Life sin's power is on the wane. God offers pardon and purity together. We cannot have one without the other. Our sins die with Christ and are buried with Him. Then, with Him, *we* must rise again.

But the old life stirs sometimes. That which is dead, cobwebbed and ghoulish, shows signs of life. Then Philippians 3:10 becomes a heart cry: *'That I may know him, and the power of his resurrection.'* Christ died, was buried and resurrected once and for all. But thank God that the miracle of resurrection *can* be repeated – *must* be repeated every day of our lives.

* * *

In His ministry Jesus raised three people from the dead.

A ruler's daughter was dying; 12 and on the threshold of womanhood. The ruler went to fetch Jesus himself; almost certainly because none of his household would go for him. His prejudice, his dignity, and his pride, were mashed into one whole wedge of humble pie as the ruler threw himself at the feet of the wandering Teacher. As they approached the house and heard the wail of flutes and scream of mourners, they were told that the girl was dead. But Jairus's daughter was snatched back from the jaws of death. What was the evidence of her resurrection? *Jesus commanded that she be given food.* The Risen Life demands the food of the Word. We must search the Scriptures to get to know their Author. *'That I may know Him,'* – for as we know Him our hearts are yielded to His Spirit, and the power of His resurrection makes us victorious.[1]

Not far from Nazareth is Nain. Nain is on the great east to west road linking the Sea of Galilee with the Mediterranean. The village of Nain is on one side of the road and its burial ground is on the other. It is possible to imagine a funeral procession coming out of Nain, headed by a band of professional mourners bearing a wicker coffin to the place of burial, crossing the great road with its camel trains. Jesus saw and heard the procession. He was moved to the depths of His heart as He saw the widow weeping for her only son. And He claimed as His own what death had seized as its prey. What was the evidence of the resurrection of the widow's son from Nain? *He began to speak.* An obvious sign of a Risen Life is witness in words to the miracle of God's grace. The Risen Life Christian is an ambassador for his Lord. He speaks for his Sovereign in an alien land.[2]

When Jesus arrived at the tomb in Bethany, Lazarus had been dead for four days. But that did not prevent his resurrection. What was the evidence of new life in Lazarus? *He walked*; though still encumbered with the clothing of death, from which Jesus told them to loose him.[3]

The Risen Life Christian must not lose his mobility in Christ by again reaching for the grave-clothes. The walk of the Risen Life is to spend each day in the company of the Risen Lord. It is an onward progress in the family of God towards the kingdom of God.

* * *

Through the Risen Life we must remember that we are not our own; our eyes, our ears, our hands, our feet, our mind are His, and we are under the weightiest obligation possible to use them to His honour and glory. And, because He died for us, this weighty obligation is our highest joy. The Risen Life is continual communion with Him. It is an application of the principles of the law of God, amplified by Jesus in the Sermon on the Mount, to every hole and corner, every jot and tittle of our lives. It is an increasing prayerfulness, an increasing sensitivity to what sin is and what duty is.

Risen Life is a growth to maturity in Jesus Christ through the power of His Spirit. The power of the Spirit yields fruit in the Risen Life. The *gifts* of the Spirit are divided unequally among believers; but *every* Risen Life, *all* born again believers are expected to have *all* the *fruits* of the Spirit. As these fruits become apparent the Risen Life believer bears 'the family likeness of the Son'.[4]

No passage of Scripture summarizes the Risen Life as well as Galatians 5:22, 23. Here the fruits of the Spirit are outlined.

The first is *love*. 'We know that we have passed from death unto life, because we love the brethren. He that loveth not his brother abideth in death.'[5] If there is no love, that tomb north of the Damascus Gate has still got a body. The so-called believer is still down among the dead men. This agape love is a self-giving love, a love that is action as well as emotion, a love that is not just for the lovable – but for those who would do us down, and it engulfs the world.

The second fruit of the Spirit is *joy*. Today's world is joyless, aimless, ruthless, full of shadows, disillusionment, and fear. But this joy is not dependent upon circumstances or upon environment. The joy of the Spirit cannot be taken away.[6]

Next comes *peace*. 'Shalom!' say the Jews in greeting. 'Salaam!' say the Arabs in greeting. Both words mean peace. The peace that is a fruit of the Spirit contains the idea of unity, completeness, rest, ease and security.

Patience; this is a difficult one. 'Lord give me patience,' a man once said, 'and be quick about it!' This patience endures ill-treatment without anger or thought of retaliation or revenge.

The fifth fruit of the Spirit is *gentleness*. The term comes from a Greek word referring to a gentleness that pervades the whole of a person's nature, banishing all that is harsh and austere. This gentleness is love enduring.

Then comes *goodness*. Goodness is love in action. It implies far more than simply 'doing good'.

Faithfulness. Fidelity in little things is one of the surest tests of a Risen Life.

Meekness is an essential for the Risen Life believer. And meekness is not weakness. It means not timid, but *tamed*. Tamed like a wild horse brought under control. A river under control can be used to generate power.

The ninth fruit of the Spirit is *self-control*. Perhaps more accurately, Spirit-control. This is the Greek word for strong, able to control thoughts and actions. Self-control, as a fruit of the Spirit, is the normal Christian life taking its exercise.

* * *

'That I may know him, and the power of his resurrection.'

These fruits of the Spirit, then, are the outgrowth of the power of His resurrection in our lives, for the power of His resurrection *is* the Holy Spirit.

We may sweat and strain to produce them for ever and a day, to end up fruitless and frustrated. ' "No branch can bear fruit by itself; it must remain in the vine. . . . apart from me you can do nothing" ', said Jesus.[7]

There is something natural and unforced about the fruits of the Spirit; they are the natural result of the life-giving sap that flows to the branch from the vine. The secret of the Risen Life, then: the vital connection with Jesus 'the Vine', spending each day in His company, 'knowing Him'. For as we know Him, as we make Him our first love and put in Him our first trust, even though we fall, He is there to help us, and, because we are looking towards Him, we become more like Him with each passing day. As we abide in Him we have the assurance that there is 'no condemnation'.[8]

* * *

'That I may know him, and the power of his resurrection.'

As we know Him and the power of His resurrection, we shall ingest the Word, that we may know Him better.

As we know Him and the power of His resurrection, we shall witness to His resurrection power and thus harness it in our lives.

As we know Him and the power of His resurrection, we shall 'come forth' as Lazarus did, reach back for our grave-clothes less and less as we walk with Him, and as the onward walk proceeds, display the fruit of His resurrection power in the manner of our living.

* * *

Death, and him that hath the power of death, then, died on the threshold of an empty tomb. That morning of Resurrection they surrendered dominion, were led captive and humbled, made, as it were, a shadow to flee before the Light shining in the darkness.

So death, and darkness and the power of sin – be not proud! For Christ the Lord, over whom none can have dominion, is risen!

Hallelujah!

1 Mark 5:21-24, 38-43. **2** Luke 7:11-15. **3** John 11:11-44. **4** Romans 8:29, Phillips. **5** 1 John 3:14. **6** John 16:22. **7** John 15:4, 5, NIV. **8** Romans 7:14-25; 8:1.

DAWN OVER GALILEE

30

At first, the indrawn breath of dark. No more. The sea beyond the veranda inaudible. Through the high, Imperial arches, just a profound blue darkness laced by skeins of starlight.

Dawn's first act commenced far in the east, over the mountains of Gergesa. The horizon hardened. A line appeared dividing sky and jagged mountain ridge, sharp as a diamond-cut on glass. Over it a dark bubble of cloud emerged. As the seconds ticked away it warmed slowly, a clinker hot with locked-in fire.

Red hot and burning it glowed. Then, all of a sudden, it caught the still unrisen sun and burst like an exploding bomb. Flares began to fall into the sea, setting it afire.

It was 5am.

Now everything happened at once. The stars snapped snut. The sky bled vermilion tides over the water. And the sun drew itself, dripping, from the waves.

The red dawn was fading.

In minutes the sounds of the daytime began, uncertainly at first.

The red dawn was gone, and the sky and sea were silver with mounting sun; the silver still framed by the black trunks of the vine-like subtropical trees that wound around the arches at the front of the Galilee hospice.

And suddenly it was day.

* * *

With the resurrection dawned a brave new world.

We had driven north from the Garden Tomb to Tabgha on Galilee. Over and around all the smooth, beautifully contoured mountains of Samaria – Ebal, Gerazim, Gilboa – we had been singing a refrain we had learned in the Garden: 'He is risen! Alleluia! He is risen! Praise the Lord!'

We even sang it around the seventeen hairpin bends to the

top of Mount Tabor. We sang it from the Carmel range, Elijah country; we sang it from the headland over Haifa where the prophet discovered that the Lord was not in the earthquake or the thunder – but the still, small voice. We sang it from Megiddo overlooking the Valley of Jezreel; apocalyptic resonances here, echoes of the last battle, the final resurrection.

Jesus is alive, accessible, our contemporary.

For this reason Christianity will always be far more than a mere philosophy or a sentiment-soaked memory. It must ever be a living relationship with a living Lord: sitting at His feet, walking by His side, kneeling in His presence, facing up to life and all that life may throw at us in the knowledge that all power in heaven and in earth is His – and that He will be with us alway, even unto the end of the world.[1]

* * *

'Bliss were it in that dawn to be alive!'

Commissioned by Jesus to go to the ends of the earth with His Gospel, the apostles were empowered by the descent of the Holy Spirit in the upper room in Jerusalem. And this descent took place at the time of the Feast of Pentecost. At Pentecost the priests presented the first loaves of the new harvest before God. The fullness of the year was gathered in. In the narrow streets of old Jerusalem, invariably animated, there was great rejoicing. The city was crammed with visitors and pilgrims. It was at the beginning of summer. Travelling conditions were at their best. Jerusalem was never more crowded than for Pentecost. The crowd – numbering some hundreds of thousands – came from distant lands. It was a time of house decoration, festal dresses and jubilant processions.

It was against this background that Peter's mighty sermon set aflying the 'winged thunderbolt of everlasting enthusiasm'.

The three crosses had been taken down.

The tomb was empty for all to see.

They had seen the wounds in hands, feet, side.

Now, from a high point on the Mount of Olives, they had seen Him break through time's hard shell, no longer to breathe earth's stale air – to sit at the right hand of God in glory, 'ever living to make intercession for us'.[2]

'Bliss were it in that dawn . . .' Jesus, a Friend in High Places, beside the eternal throne. With that truth burning inside they could face the magistrate, the provincial govenor, even imperial Caesar. It was an all-conquering faith, more than enough to confront magic, witchcraft and paganism. It was a singing faith with which to encounter imprisonment, fire, sword and lions. It was a glorious faith – enough to outface death, and the father of terrors himself. Beside the eternal throne of power, judgement, destiny, stood Jesus, their Friend – *stands Jesus, our Friend* – 'a merciful High Priest, touched with the feeling of our infirmities',[3] Advocate with the Father, only Mediator between man and God.

But even that was not all that made hearts leap as the early crusaders for Christ descended the slopes of the Mount of Olives, following the ascension, to await the descent of the Spirit. The heavenly messengers, attendant upon the ascension, had echoed a promise repeated many times by Jesus: 'This same Jesus which is taken up from you into heaven, shall so come in like manner as ye have seen him go . . . .'[4] *This same Jesus* – Who had lain among the sharp straws of a Bethlehem manger, Who had taught sublime truths in the synagogue at Capernaum, Who had healed bodies and minds by the inland sea, Who had taken a little child upon His knee.

Even before the New Testament was written, when the Church gathered around the Lord's table to 'show the Lord's death till He come' their greeting – untranslated from the mother tongue of Christianity – was 'Maranatha': 'Lord, come!' And they would recall the words of their glorified Lord: 'Blessed are those servants, whom the lord when he cometh shall find watching: . . . Be ye therefore ready also: for the Son of man cometh at an hour when ye think not.'[5]

* * *

We sat in silence by the shoreline at Tabgha. For one last time we listened to the sob of the brimming water of the lake and, in fancy, heard the echo of events long past whisper across the silence.

One last moment of intimacy; the Risen Lord and the eleven before the ascension.

They went before Him into Galilee. While the lake was dimpling in the warm sunset they put out to fish. In the profound blue darkness laced with starlight nothing was to be heard save the letting out and the drawing in of nets, or the occasional stroke of the oar. When the flares from the still unrisen sun set the sea on fire, they had caught nothing. As the red faded, they failed to recognize the figure standing on the Tabgha shingle enwrapped in the silver shimmer of morning mist. At His instruction the net was recast, and drawn in bursting with fish.

When day dawned – in response to His invitation 'Come and dine' – they were crouching around a fire He had built at the water's edge, eating a fish breakfast prepared by His hands.[6]

Their future was not in these waters but by fires He would light and meals His hands would prepare.

Through the prints of the nails in the hands and feet, clearly visible in the sudden dawn; through the conquest of death He had accomplished, and the empty tomb He left behind, salvation, sweet peace, unbounded joy and heaven were on offer to all men.

This was, at once, their message and their hope.

Those who grasp what He offers with the empty hand of faith will hear His voice saying, 'Come and dine', and, like the eleven, meet Him again on the shores of another sea: the sea of glass whose placid waters are red with the mingled fire of an eternal sunrise.[7]

1 Matthew 28:18-20. **2** Hebrews 1:3; 9:24; See 7:25. **3** See Hebrews 4:15. See also R. E. O. White, *The Stranger of Galilee*, page 168. **4** Acts 1:10-12. **5** Luke 12:37-40; R. E. O. White, op cit, page 201. **6** John 21. **7** Revelation 4:6; 15:2.